# Monthly Treasury Statement

## of Receipts and Outlays
## of the United States Government

For Fiscal Year 2014 Through **May 31, 2014**, and Other Periods

### Highlight

**Outlays for Military active duty and retirement, Veterans' benefits, Supplemental Security Income, and Medicare payments to Health Maintenance Organizations and prescription drug plans accelerate into May since June 1, the normal payment date, falls on a non-business day.**

**Receipts, Outlays, and Surplus/Deficit for May 2014**
[ $billions ]

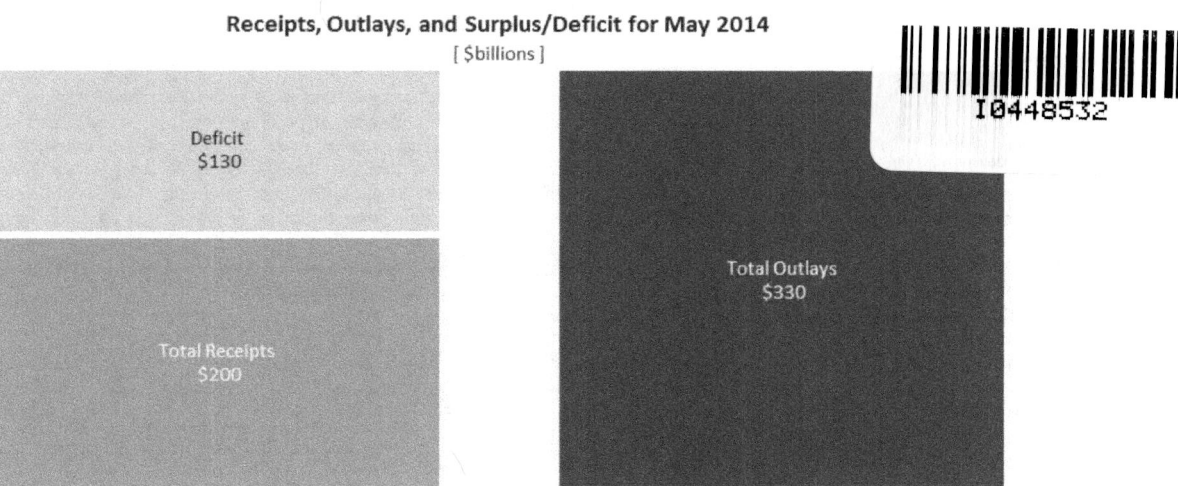

Deficit $130

Total Receipts $200

Total Outlays $330

**Receipts, Outlays, and Surplus/Deficit through Fiscal Year 2014**
[ $billions ]

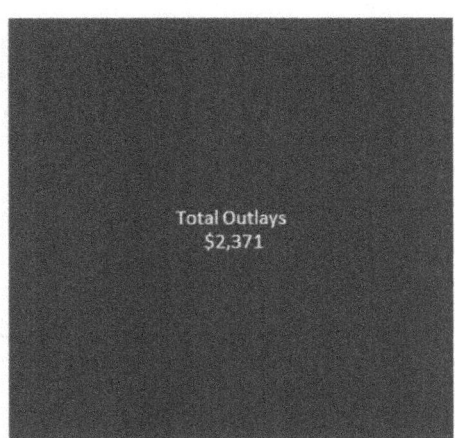

Deficit $436

Total Receipts $1,935

Total Outlays $2,371

Compiled and Published by
## *Department of the Treasury*
## **Bureau of the Fiscal Service**

# Contents

# Introduction

*The Monthly Treasury Statement of Receipts and Outlays of the United States Government (MTS)* is prepared by the Bureau of the Fiscal Service, Department of the Treasury, and after approval by the Fiscal Assistant Secretary of the Treasury, is normally released on the 8th workday of the month following the reporting month. The publication is based on data provided by Federal entities, disbursing officers, and Federal Reserve banks.

## AUDIENCE

The *MTS* is published to meet the needs of those responsible for or interested in the cash position of the Treasury, those who are responsible or interested in the Government's budget results, and individuals and businesses whose operations depend upon or are related to the Government's financial operations.

## DISCLOSURE STATEMENT

This statement summarizes the financial activities of the Federal Government and off-budget Federal entities conducted in accordance with the Budget of the U.S. Government, i.e., receipts and outlays of funds, the surplus or deficit, and the means of financing the deficit or disposing of the surplus. Information is presented on a modified cash basis; receipts are accounted for on the basis of collections; refunds of receipts are treated as deductions from gross receipts; revolving and management fund receipts, reimbursements and refunds of monies previously expended are treated as deductions from gross outlays; and interest on the public debt (public issues) is recognized on the accrual basis. Major information sources include accounting data reported by Federal entities, disbursing officers, and Federal Reserve banks.

## TRIAD OF PUBLICATIONS

The *MTS* is part of a triad of Treasury financial reports. The *Daily Treasury Statement* is published each working day of the Federal Government. It provides data on the cash and debt operations of the Treasury based upon reporting of the Treasury account balances by Federal Reserve banks. The *MTS* is a report of Government receipts and outlays based on agency reporting. The *Combined Statement of Receipts, Outlays, and Balances of the United States Government* is the official publication of the detailed receipts and outlays of the Government. It is published annually in accordance with legislative mandates given to the Secretary of the Treasury.

## DATA SOURCES AND INFORMATION

The Explanatory Notes section of this publication provides information concerning the flow of data into the *MTS* and sources of information relevant to the *MTS*.

## Table 1. Summary of Receipts, Outlays, and the Deficit/Surplus of the U.S. Government, Fiscal Years 2013 and 2014, by Month

[$ millions]

| Period | Receipts | Outlays | Deficit/Surplus (-) |
|---|---|---|---|
| **FY 2013** | | | |
| October | 184,316 | 304,311 | 119,995 |
| November | 161,730 | 333,841 | 172,112 |
| December | 269,508 | 270,699 | 1,191 |
| January | 272,225 | 269,340 | -2,886 |
| February | 122,815 | 326,354 | 203,539 |
| March | 186,018 | 292,548 | 106,530 |
| April | 406,723 | 293,834 | -112,889 |
| May | 197,182 | 335,914 | 138,732 |
| June | 286,627 | 170,126 | -116,501 |
| July | 200,030 | 297,627 | 97,597 |
| August | 185,370 | 333,293 | 147,923 |
| September | 301,469 | 226,355 | -75,114 |
| Year-to-Date | ¹2,774,011 | ¹3,454,241 | ¹680,229 |
| **FY 2014** | | | |
| October | 198,927 | 289,511 | 90,584 |
| November | 182,453 | 317,679 | 135,226 |
| December | 283,221 | 230,001 | -53,220 |
| January | 295,997 | 306,247 | 10,250 |
| February | 144,349 | 337,880 | 193,532 |
| March | 215,846 | 252,739 | 36,893 |
| April | 414,237 | 307,383 | -106,853 |
| May | 199,889 | 329,860 | 129,971 |
| Year-to-Date | 1,934,919 | 2,371,301 | 436,382 |

¹The receipt, outlay and deficit figures differ from the *FY 2015 Budget*, released by the Office of Management and Budget on March 4, 2014. The deficit figure differs by -$727 million, due mainly to revisions in the data following the release of the Final Monthly Treasury Statement.

Note: Details may not add to totals due to rounding.

## Table 2. Summary of Budget and Off-Budget Results and Financing of the U.S. Government, May 2014 and Other Periods
[$ millions]

| Classification | This Month | Current Fiscal Year to Date | Budget Estimates Full Fiscal Year[1] | Prior Fiscal Year to Date (2013) | Budget Estimates Next Fiscal Year (2015)[1] |
|---|---|---|---|---|---|
| Total On-Budget and Off-Budget Results: | | | | | |
| Total Receipts | 199,889 | 1,934,919 | 3,001,721 | 1,800,515 | 3,337,425 |
| On-Budget Receipts | 140,789 | 1,441,203 | 2,269,389 | 1,361,277 | 2,579,548 |
| Off-Budget Receipts | 59,100 | 493,716 | 732,332 | 439,239 | 757,877 |
| Total Outlays | 329,860 | 2,371,301 | 3,650,526 | 2,426,840 | 3,900,989 |
| On-Budget Outlays | 260,468 | 1,892,407 | 2,939,299 | 2,007,834 | 3,143,368 |
| Off-Budget Outlays | 69,392 | 478,894 | 711,227 | 419,006 | 757,621 |
| Total Surplus (+) or Deficit (-) | -129,971 | -436,382 | -648,805 | -626,325 | -563,564 |
| On-Budget Surplus (+) or Deficit (-) | -119,679 | -451,204 | -669,910 | -646,558 | -563,820 |
| Off-Budget Surplus (+) or Deficit (-) | -10,292 | +14,822 | +21,105 | +20,233 | +256 |
| Total On-Budget and Off-Budget Financing | 129,971 | 436,382 | 648,805 | 626,325 | 563,564 |
| Means of Financing: | | | | | |
| Borrowing from the Public | 34,692 | 552,208 | 920,083 | 631,896 | 689,142 |
| Reduction of Operating Cash, Increase (-) | 119,449 | 59,492 | -1,614 | 50,765 | ...... |
| By Other Means | -24,170 | -175,319 | -269,664 | -56,336 | -125,578 |

[1]These estimates are based on the *FY 2015 Budget*, released by the Office of Management and Budget on March 4, 2014.

... No Transactions

Note: Details may not add to totals due to rounding.

## Figure 1. Monthly Receipts, Outlays, and Budget Deficit/Surplus of the U.S. Government, Fiscal Years 2013 and 2014

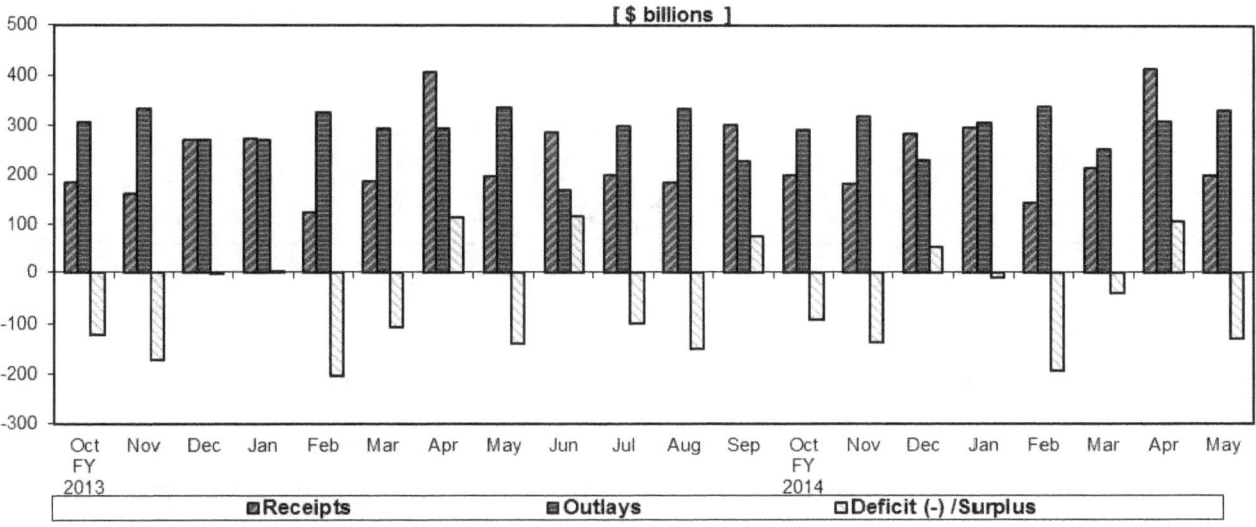

## Figure 2. Cumulative Monthly Receipts, Outlays, and Budget Deficit/Surplus of the U.S. Government, Fiscal Years 2013 and 2014

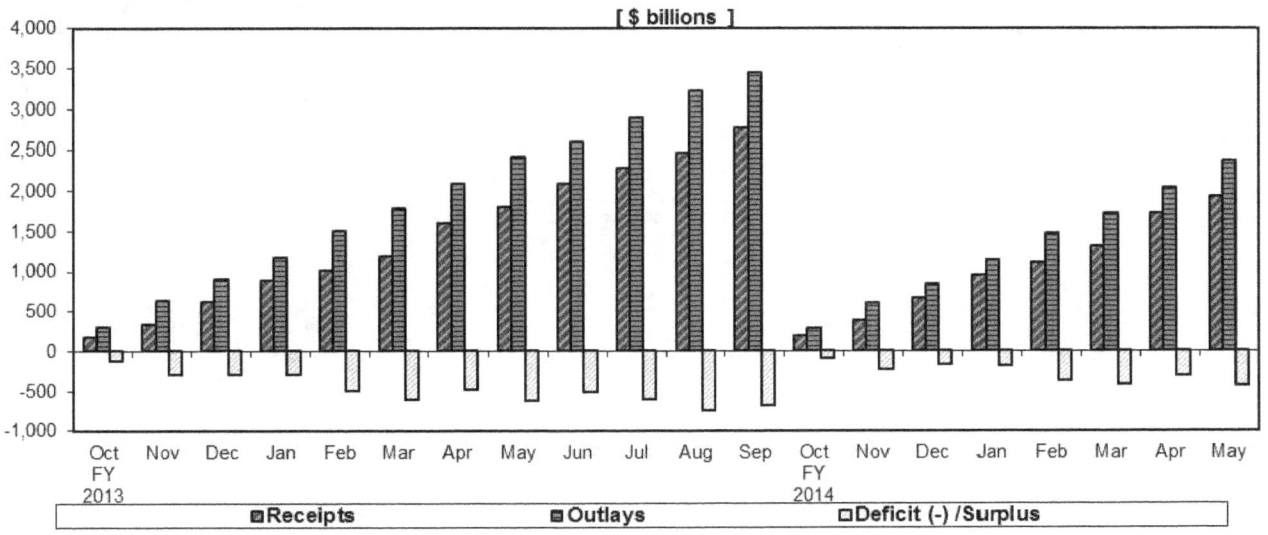

Figure 3. Monthly Receipts of the U.S. Government, by Source, Fiscal Years 2013 and 2014

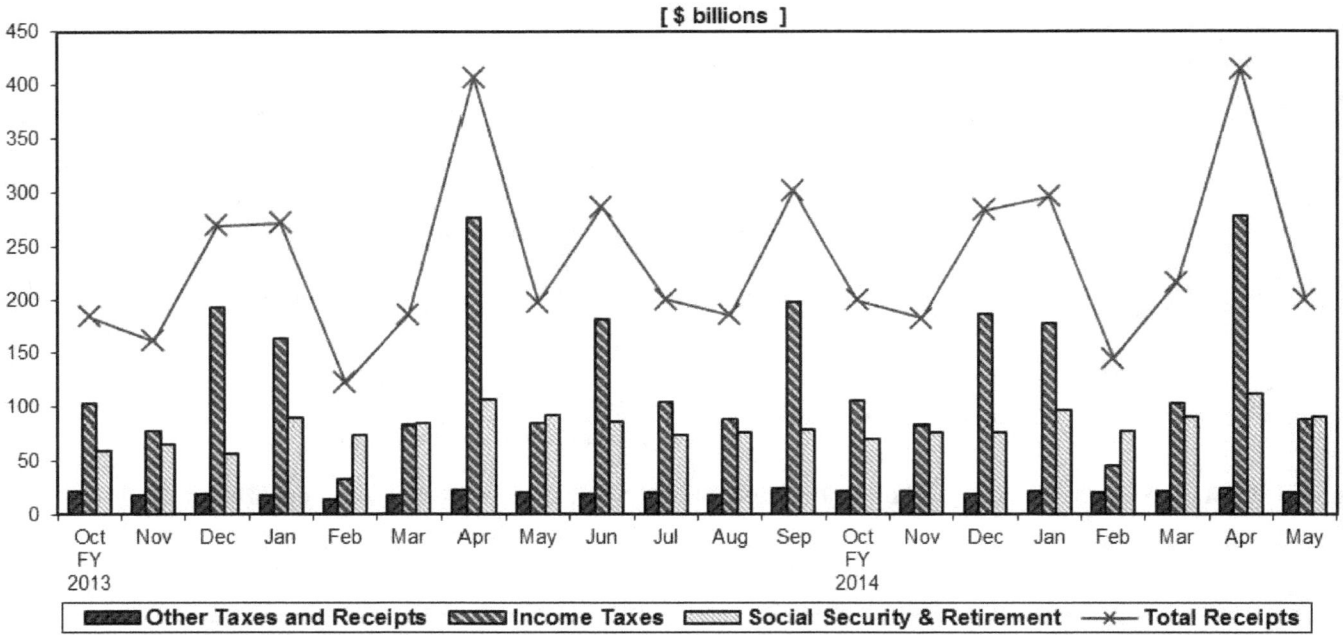

Figure 4. Monthly Outlays of the U.S. Government, by Function, Fiscal Years 2013 and 2014

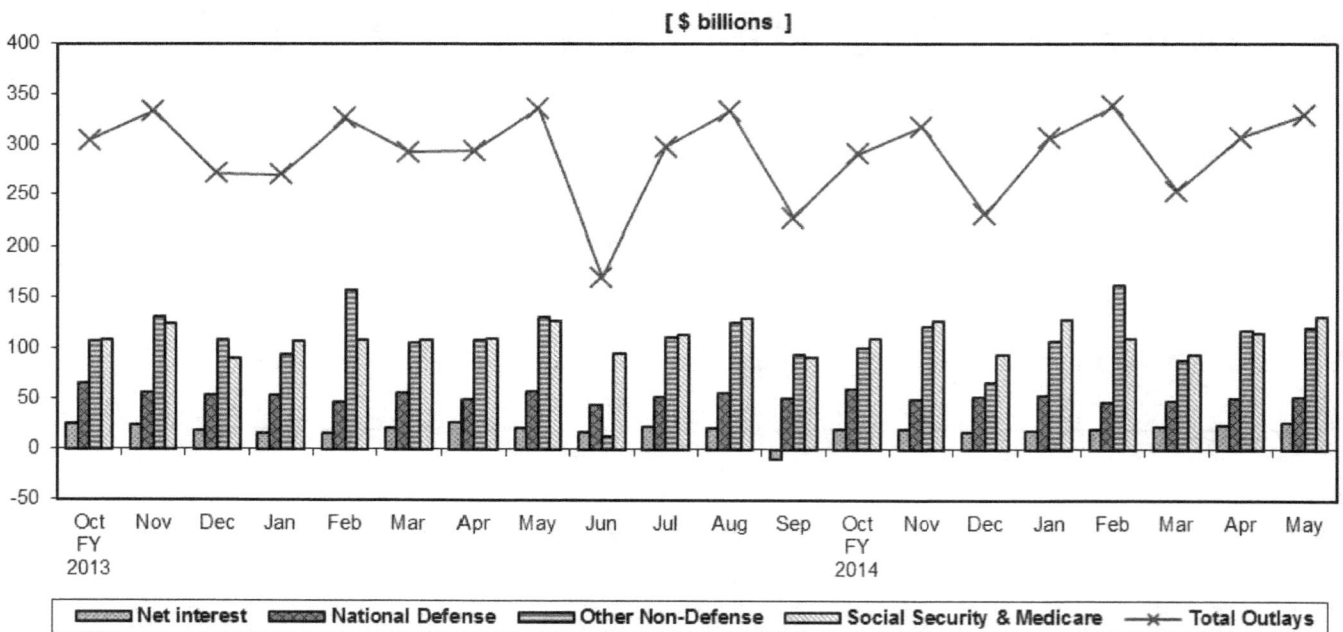

## Table 3. Summary of Receipts and Outlays of the U.S. Government, May 2014 and Other Periods
[$ millions]

| Classification | This Month | Current Fiscal Year to Date | Comparable Prior Period Year to Date | Budget Estimates Full Fiscal Year[1] |
|---|---|---|---|---|
| **Budget Receipts** | | | | |
| Individual Income Taxes | 79,945 | 903,024 | 873,862 | 1,386,068 |
| Corporation Income Taxes | 8,031 | 164,840 | 142,632 | 332,740 |
| Social Insurance and Retirement Receipts: | | | | |
| Employment and General Retirement (Off-Budget) | 59,100 | 493,716 | 439,239 | 732,332 |
| Employment and General Retirement (On-Budget) | 16,568 | 155,027 | 142,556 | 224,619 |
| Unemployment Insurance | 15,591 | 43,231 | 45,605 | 60,393 |
| Other Retirement | 311 | 2,294 | 2,398 | 3,765 |
| Excise Taxes | 5,697 | 51,563 | 52,650 | 93,528 |
| Estate and Gift Taxes | 1,432 | 12,582 | 13,720 | 15,746 |
| Customs Duties | 2,434 | 22,125 | 20,568 | 34,966 |
| Miscellaneous Receipts | 10,781 | 86,517 | 67,287 | 117,564 |
| **Total Receipts** | **199,889** | **1,934,919** | **1,800,515** | **3,001,721** |
| (On-Budget) | 140,789 | 1,441,203 | 1,361,277 | 2,269,389 |
| (Off-Budget) | 59,100 | 493,716 | 439,239 | 732,332 |
| **Budget Outlays** | | | | |
| Legislative Branch | 337 | 2,716 | 2,976 | 4,740 |
| Judicial Branch | 534 | 4,496 | 4,762 | 7,281 |
| Department of Agriculture | 10,018 | 100,695 | 114,383 | 149,191 |
| Department of Commerce | 623 | 5,144 | 6,160 | 8,213 |
| Department of Defense-Military Programs | 48,891 | 390,300 | 415,390 | 593,343 |
| Department of Education | 5,164 | 36,000 | 36,294 | 65,619 |
| Department of Energy | 1,710 | 15,543 | 16,449 | 27,773 |
| Department of Health and Human Services | 95,432 | 623,990 | 606,433 | 957,978 |
| Department of Homeland Security | 3,074 | 27,798 | 41,206 | 51,628 |
| Department of Housing and Urban Development | 1,042 | 26,410 | 21,339 | 42,121 |
| Department of the Interior | 788 | 7,193 | 5,117 | 12,834 |
| Department of Justice | 1,975 | 17,158 | 20,429 | 28,651 |
| Department of Labor | 4,376 | 40,470 | 57,254 | 76,507 |
| Department of State | 1,650 | 17,196 | 16,088 | 27,770 |
| Department of Transportation | 4,976 | 45,766 | 46,532 | 80,531 |
| Department of the Treasury: | | | | |
| Interest on Treasury Debt Securities (Gross) | 32,081 | 256,054 | 252,230 | 427,219 |
| Other | 6,483 | 43,600 | 81,839 | 41,937 |
| Department of Veterans Affairs | 17,596 | 104,682 | 95,198 | 150,682 |
| Corps of Engineers | 622 | 4,387 | 4,446 | 7,153 |
| Other Defense Civil Programs | 8,398 | 42,701 | 41,791 | 57,877 |
| Environmental Protection Agency | 624 | 5,581 | 6,607 | 8,128 |
| Executive Office of the President | 30 | 244 | 252 | 392 |
| General Services Administration | 80 | -107 | -118 | -477 |
| International Assistance Program | 1,687 | 12,516 | 12,609 | 20,359 |
| National Aeronautics and Space Administration | 1,344 | 11,069 | 11,044 | 17,063 |
| National Science Foundation | 520 | 4,184 | 4,483 | 7,051 |
| Office of Personnel Management | 6,929 | 58,826 | 55,920 | 92,419 |
| Small Business Administration | 86 | -121 | 57 | 365 |
| Social Security Administration | 80,291 | 601,322 | 575,170 | 914,368 |
| Other Independent Agencies | 1,813 | 5,775 | 18,899 | 18,717 |
| Allowances | ..... | ..... | ..... | 1,875 |
| Undistributed Offsetting Receipts: | | | | |
| Interest | -3,340 | -79,194 | -76,962 | -158,042 |
| Other | -5,971 | -61,094 | -67,436 | -90,740 |
| **Total Outlays** | **329,860** | **2,371,301** | **2,426,840** | **3,650,526** |
| (On-Budget) | 260,468 | 1,892,407 | 2,007,834 | 2,939,299 |
| (Off-Budget) | 69,392 | 478,894 | 419,006 | 711,227 |
| **Surplus (+) or Deficit (-)** | **-129,971** | **-436,382** | **-626,325** | **-648,805** |
| (On-Budget) | -119,679 | -451,204 | -646,558 | -669,910 |
| (Off-Budget) | -10,292 | +14,822 | +20,233 | +21,105 |

[1]These estimates are based on the *FY 2015 Budget*, released by the Office of Management and Budget on March 4, 2014.

... No Transactions

Note: Details may not add to totals due to rounding.

## Table 4. Receipts of the U.S. Government, May 2014 and Other Periods
[$ millions]

| Classification | This Month | | | Current Fiscal Year to Date | | | Prior Fiscal Year to Date | | |
|---|---|---|---|---|---|---|---|---|---|
| | Gross Receipts | Refunds (Deduct) | Receipts | Gross Receipts | Refunds (Deduct) | Receipts | Gross Receipts | Refunds (Deduct) | Receipts |
| **Individual Income Taxes:** | | | | | | | | | |
| Withheld | 86,829 | | | 785,473 | | | 766,826 | | |
| Presidential Election Campaign Fund | 6 | | | 27 | | | 33 | | |
| Other | 6,582 | | | 333,226 | | | 321,982 | | |
| Total--Individual Income Taxes | 93,418 | 13,473 | 79,945 | 1,118,726 | 215,702 | 903,024 | 1,088,841 | 214,979 | 873,862 |
| **Corporation Income Taxes** | 9,371 | 1,339 | 8,031 | 190,084 | 25,244 | 164,840 | 173,629 | 30,997 | 142,632 |
| **Social Insurance and Retirement Receipts:** | | | | | | | | | |
| Employment and General Retirement: | | | | | | | | | |
| Federal Old-Age and Survivors Ins. Trust Fund: | | | | | | | | | |
| Federal Insurance Contributions Act Taxes | 49,769 | ...... | 49,769 | 393,669 | ...... | 393,669 | 357,263 | ...... | 357,263 |
| Self-Employment Contributions Act Taxes | 752 | ...... | 752 | 24,903 | ...... | 24,903 | 20,206 | ...... | 20,206 |
| Adjustments Attributable to Prior Years | (**) | ...... | (**) | 3,480 | ...... | 3,480 | -1,984 | ...... | -1,984 |
| Total--FOASI Trust Fund | 50,521 | ...... | 50,521 | 422,052 | ...... | 422,052 | 375,485 | ...... | 375,485 |
| Federal Disability Insurance Trust Fund: | | | | | | | | | |
| Federal Insurance Contributions Act Taxes | 8,451 | ...... | 8,451 | 66,848 | ...... | 66,848 | 60,673 | ...... | 60,673 |
| Self-Employment Contributions Act Taxes | 128 | ...... | 128 | 4,231 | ...... | 4,231 | 3,430 | ...... | 3,430 |
| Adjustments Attributable to Prior Years | ...... | ...... | ...... | 586 | ...... | 586 | -349 | ...... | -349 |
| Total--FDI Trust Fund | 8,579 | ...... | 8,579 | 71,665 | ...... | 71,665 | 63,754 | ...... | 63,754 |
| Federal Hospital Insurance Trust Fund: | | | | | | | | | |
| Federal Insurance Contributions Act Taxes | 15,749 | ...... | 15,749 | 137,605 | ...... | 137,605 | 129,396 | ...... | 129,396 |
| Self-Employment Contributions Act Taxes | 339 | ...... | 339 | 11,496 | ...... | 11,496 | 10,264 | ...... | 10,264 |
| Adjustments Attributable to Prior Years | ...... | ...... | ...... | 1,974 | ...... | 1,974 | -806 | ...... | -806 |
| Total--FHI Trust Fund | 16,088 | ...... | 16,088 | 151,075 | ...... | 151,075 | 138,854 | ...... | 138,854 |
| Railroad Retirement : | | | | | | | | | |
| Rail Pension and Supplemental Annuity | 256 | 1 | 255 | 2,021 | 8 | 2,013 | 1,922 | 31 | 1,891 |
| Social Security Equivalent Account | 226 | 1 | 225 | 1,947 | 8 | 1,939 | 1,843 | 32 | 1,811 |
| Total--Employment and General Retirement | 75,670 | 2 | 75,668 | 648,759 | 16 | 648,743 | 581,858 | 63 | 581,795 |
| Unemployment Insurance: | | | | | | | | | |
| Deposits by States | 15,462 | ...... | 15,462 | 35,640 | ...... | 35,640 | 38,599 | ...... | 38,599 |
| Federal Unemployment Tax Act Taxes | 144 | 17 | 127 | 7,655 | 91 | 7,564 | 7,002 | 96 | 6,905 |
| Railroad Unemployment Taxes | 2 | ...... | 2 | 27 | ...... | 27 | 101 | ...... | 101 |
| Total--Unemployment Insurance | 15,608 | 17 | 15,591 | 43,322 | 91 | 43,231 | 45,702 | 96 | 45,605 |
| Other Retirement: | | | | | | | | | |
| Federal Employees Retirement - Employee Share | 309 | ...... | 309 | 2,277 | ...... | 2,277 | 2,380 | ...... | 2,380 |
| Non-Federal Employees Retirement | 2 | ...... | 2 | 17 | ...... | 17 | 18 | ...... | 18 |
| Total--Other Retirement | 311 | ...... | 311 | 2,294 | ...... | 2,294 | 2,398 | ...... | 2,398 |
| Total--Social Insurance and Retirement Receipts | 91,589 | 19 | 91,570 | 694,375 | 107 | 694,268 | 629,958 | 160 | 629,798 |
| **Excise Taxes:** | | | | | | | | | |
| Miscellaneous Excise Taxes | 2,553 | 1,499 | 1,054 | 22,093 | 2,632 | 19,461 | 22,290 | 1,426 | 20,864 |
| Airport and Airway Trust Fund | 1,229 | 4 | 1,224 | 8,137 | 10 | 8,126 | 8,216 | 7 | 8,209 |
| Highway Trust Fund | 3,371 | ...... | 3,371 | 23,609 | ...... | 23,609 | 23,213 | ...... | 23,213 |
| Black Lung Disability Trust Fund | 48 | ...... | 48 | 367 | ...... | 367 | 365 | ...... | 365 |
| Total--Excise Taxes | 7,200 | 1,503 | 5,697 | 54,205 | 2,642 | 51,563 | 54,083 | 1,433 | 52,650 |
| **Estate and Gift Taxes** | 1,478 | 47 | 1,432 | 13,124 | 542 | 12,582 | 14,446 | 726 | 13,720 |
| **Customs Duties** | 2,537 | 103 | 2,434 | 23,005 | 880 | 22,125 | 21,434 | 866 | 20,568 |
| **Miscellaneous Receipts:** | | | | | | | | | |
| Deposits of Earnings by Federal Reserve Banks | 8,331 | ...... | 8,331 | 66,200 | ...... | 66,200 | 49,410 | ...... | 49,410 |
| Universal Service Fund | 838 | ...... | 838 | 6,559 | ...... | 6,559 | 6,636 | ...... | 6,636 |
| All Other | 1,614 | 2 | 1,612 | 13,780 | 22 | 13,759 | 11,263 | 22 | 11,241 |
| Total -- Miscellaneous Receipts | 10,783 | 2 | 10,781 | 86,539 | 22 | 86,517 | 67,308 | 22 | 67,287 |
| **Total -- Receipts** | 216,376 | 16,487 | 199,889 | 2,180,057 | 245,138 | 1,934,919 | 2,049,700 | 249,184 | 1,800,515 |
| Total -- On-Budget | 157,276 | 16,487 | 140,789 | 1,686,341 | 245,138 | 1,441,203 | 1,610,461 | 249,184 | 1,361,277 |
| Total -- Off-Budget | 59,100 | ...... | 59,100 | 493,716 | ...... | 493,716 | 439,239 | ...... | 439,239 |

... No Transactions
(**) Less than $500,000

Note: Details may not add to totals due to rounding.

| Classification | This Month | | | Current Fiscal Year to Date | | | Prior Fiscal Year to Date | | |
|---|---|---|---|---|---|---|---|---|---|
| | Gross Outlays | Applicable Receipts | Outlays | Gross Outlays | Applicable Receipts | Outlays | Gross Outlays | Applicable Receipts | Outlays |
| **Legislative Branch:** | | | | | | | | | |
| Senate | 65 | (**) | 64 | 536 | 2 | 534 | 577 | 2 | 574 |
| House of Representatives | 99 | (**) | 98 | 823 | 2 | 821 | 856 | 2 | 854 |
| Joint Items | 1 | ...... | 1 | 10 | ...... | 10 | 12 | ...... | 12 |
| Capitol Police | 26 | ...... | 26 | 209 | ...... | 209 | 235 | ...... | 235 |
| Congressional Budget Office | 3 | ...... | 3 | 27 | ...... | 27 | 29 | ...... | 29 |
| Architect of the Capitol | 42 | 1 | 41 | 284 | 3 | 282 | 363 | 3 | 360 |
| Library of Congress | 44 | 1 | 43 | 367 | 6 | 361 | 427 | 6 | 421 |
| Government Printing Office | 10 | ...... | 10 | 97 | ...... | 97 | 105 | ...... | 105 |
| Government Accountability Office | 38 | ...... | 38 | 321 | ...... | 321 | 326 | ...... | 326 |
| United States Tax Court | 8 | ...... | 8 | 36 | ...... | 36 | 33 | ...... | 33 |
| Other Legislative Branch Agencies | 5 | ...... | 5 | 35 | ...... | 35 | 40 | ...... | 40 |
| Proprietary Receipts from the Public | ...... | 2 | -2 | ...... | 12 | -12 | ...... | 6 | -6 |
| Intrabudgetary Transaction | (**) | ...... | (**) | -6 | ...... | -6 | -8 | ...... | -8 |
| Offsetting Governmental Receipts | ...... | ...... | ...... | ...... | (**) | (**) | ...... | (**) | (**) |
| Total--Legislative Branch | 340 | 3 | 337 | 2,739 | 24 | 2,716 | 2,995 | 19 | 2,976 |
| **Judicial Branch:** | | | | | | | | | |
| Supreme Court of the United States | 7 | ...... | 7 | 66 | ...... | 66 | 55 | ...... | 55 |
| Courts of Appeals, District Courts, and Other | | | | | | | | | |
| Judicial Services | 536 | ...... | 536 | 4,681 | ...... | 4,681 | 4,893 | ...... | 4,893 |
| Other | 12 | ...... | 12 | 326 | ...... | 326 | 215 | ...... | 215 |
| Proprietary Receipts from the Public | ...... | 21 | -21 | ...... | 109 | -109 | ...... | 111 | -111 |
| Intrabudgetary Transactions | -1 | ...... | -1 | -467 | ...... | -467 | -291 | ...... | -291 |
| Total--Judicial Branch | 555 | 21 | 534 | 4,605 | 109 | 4,496 | 4,872 | 111 | 4,762 |
| **Department of Agriculture:** | | | | | | | | | |
| Agricultural Research Service | 88 | ...... | 88 | 679 | ...... | 679 | 742 | ...... | 742 |
| National Institute of Food and Agriculture: | | | | | | | | | |
| Research and Education Activities | 42 | ...... | 42 | 412 | ...... | 412 | 395 | ...... | 395 |
| Extension Activities | 21 | ...... | 21 | 275 | ...... | 275 | 211 | ...... | 211 |
| Other | 9 | ...... | 9 | 67 | ...... | 67 | 79 | ...... | 79 |
| Animal and Plant Health Inspection Service | 81 | ...... | 81 | 657 | ...... | 657 | 697 | ...... | 697 |
| Food Safety and Inspection Service | 88 | ...... | 88 | 632 | ...... | 632 | 670 | ...... | 670 |
| Agricultural Marketing Service | 71 | ...... | 71 | 491 | ...... | 491 | 698 | ...... | 698 |
| Risk Management Agency: | | | | | | | | | |
| Administrative and Operating Expenses | 4 | ...... | 4 | 41 | ...... | 41 | 48 | ...... | 48 |
| Federal Crop Insurance Corporation Fund | 233 | 27 | 206 | 9,808 | 179 | 9,629 | 16,980 | 2,432 | 14,548 |
| Farm Service Agency: | | | | | | | | | |
| Salaries and Expenses | 139 | ...... | 139 | 603 | ...... | 603 | 963 | ...... | 963 |
| USDA Supplemental Assistance | (**) | ...... | (**) | (**) | ...... | (**) | (**) | ...... | (**) |
| Agricultural Disaster Relief Fund | 1 | ...... | 1 | 34 | ...... | 34 | 1,419 | ...... | 1,419 |
| Commodity Credit Corporation | 577 | 653 | -77 | 14,150 | 4,872 | 9,278 | 17,111 | 7,687 | 9,424 |
| Tobacco Trust Fund | 1 | ...... | 1 | 620 | ...... | 620 | 434 | ...... | 434 |
| Agricultural Credit Insurance Fund | 10 | 7 | 3 | 560 | 95 | 465 | 71 | 133 | -62 |
| Other | 13 | ...... | 13 | 34 | ...... | 34 | 41 | ...... | 41 |
| Total--Farm Service Agency | 742 | 660 | 82 | 16,002 | 4,967 | 11,035 | 20,039 | 7,820 | 12,219 |
| Natural Resources Conservation Service: | | | | | | | | | |
| Conservation Operations | 61 | ...... | 61 | 494 | ...... | 494 | 545 | ...... | 545 |
| Farm Security and Rural Investment Programs | 132 | ...... | 132 | 2,064 | ...... | 2,064 | 2,042 | ...... | 2,042 |
| Other | 10 | ...... | 10 | 85 | ...... | 85 | 116 | ...... | 116 |
| Rural Development | 54 | ...... | 54 | -65 | ...... | -65 | 20 | ...... | 20 |
| Rural Housing Service: | | | | | | | | | |
| Rural Housing Insurance Fund | 5 | 40 | -35 | 463 | 363 | 101 | 459 | 417 | 42 |
| Rental Assistance Program | 96 | ...... | 96 | 775 | ...... | 775 | 758 | ...... | 758 |
| Other | 10 | ...... | 10 | 81 | ...... | 81 | 106 | ...... | 106 |
| Rural Utilities Service: | | | | | | | | | |
| Rural Electrification and Telecommunications Fund | 808 | 1,100 | -292 | 982 | 2,270 | -1,287 | 199 | 672 | -473 |
| Other | 76 | 14 | 61 | 658 | 122 | 536 | 988 | 143 | 846 |
| Foreign Agricultural Service | 192 | ...... | 192 | 949 | ...... | 949 | 1,295 | ...... | 1,295 |
| Food and Nutrition Service: | | | | | | | | | |
| Supplemental Nutrition Assistance Program | 6,285 | ...... | 6,285 | 51,038 | ...... | 51,038 | 55,311 | ...... | 55,311 |
| Child Nutrition Programs | 1,953 | ...... | 1,953 | 14,544 | ...... | 14,544 | 14,748 | ...... | 14,748 |
| Special Supplemental Nutrition Program for Women, Infants, and Children (WIC) | 531 | ...... | 531 | 4,169 | ...... | 4,169 | 4,447 | ...... | 4,447 |
| Other | 31 | ...... | 31 | 220 | ...... | 220 | 312 | ...... | 312 |
| Total--Food and Nutrition Service | 8,799 | ...... | 8,799 | 69,971 | ...... | 69,971 | 74,819 | ...... | 74,819 |
| Forest Service: | | | | | | | | | |
| National Forest System | 133 | ...... | 133 | 959 | ...... | 959 | 965 | ...... | 965 |
| Capital Improvement and Maintenance | 25 | ...... | 25 | 209 | ...... | 209 | 277 | ...... | 277 |
| Wildland Fire Management | 157 | ...... | 157 | 1,351 | ...... | 1,351 | 1,471 | ...... | 1,471 |
| Forest Service Permanent Appropriations | 4 | ...... | 4 | 362 | ...... | 362 | 411 | ...... | 411 |
| Other | 53 | ...... | 53 | 521 | ...... | 521 | 589 | ...... | 589 |
| Total--Forest Service | 373 | ...... | 373 | 3,401 | ...... | 3,401 | 3,714 | ...... | 3,714 |
| Other | 66 | 4 | 62 | 664 | 40 | 625 | 758 | 30 | 728 |
| Proprietary Receipts from the Public | ...... | 143 | -143 | ...... | 1,039 | -1,039 | ...... | 721 | -721 |
| Intrabudgetary Transactions | -56 | ...... | -56 | 85 | ...... | 85 | 239 | ...... | 239 |
| Total--Department of Agriculture | 12,006 | 1,988 | 10,018 | 109,673 | 8,979 | 100,695 | 126,616 | 12,234 | 114,383 |

## Table 5. Outlays of the U.S. Government, May 2014 and Other Periods —Continued
[$ millions]

| Classification | This Month Gross Outlays | This Month Applicable Receipts | This Month Outlays | Current Fiscal Year to Date Gross Outlays | Current Fiscal Year to Date Applicable Receipts | Current Fiscal Year to Date Outlays | Prior Fiscal Year to Date Gross Outlays | Prior Fiscal Year to Date Applicable Receipts | Prior Fiscal Year to Date Outlays |
|---|---|---|---|---|---|---|---|---|---|
| **Department of Commerce:** | | | | | | | | | |
| Economic Development Administration | 34 | (**) | 34 | 238 | 1 | 236 | 317 | (**) | 316 |
| Bureau of the Census | 78 | ...... | 78 | 694 | ...... | 694 | 756 | ...... | 756 |
| International Trade Administration | 32 | ...... | 32 | 280 | ...... | 280 | 298 | ...... | 298 |
| National Oceanic and Atmospheric Administration | 427 | 15 | 412 | 3,480 | 147 | 3,333 | 3,547 | 84 | 3,463 |
| National Institute of Standards and Technology | 65 | ...... | 65 | 538 | ...... | 538 | 629 | ...... | 629 |
| National Telecommunication and Information Administration | 1 | ...... | 1 | 274 | ...... | 274 | 707 | ...... | 707 |
| Other | 12 | 8 | 4 | -138 | 64 | -202 | 64 | 47 | 17 |
| Proprietary Receipts from the Public | ...... | 4 | -4 | ...... | 3 | -3 | ...... | 29 | -29 |
| Intrabudgetary Transactions | 1 | ...... | 1 | -6 | ...... | -6 | 2 | ...... | 2 |
| Offsetting Governmental Receipts | ...... | (**) | (**) | ...... | 2 | -2 | ...... | 2 | -2 |
| **Total--Department of Commerce** | 651 | 28 | 623 | 5,360 | 216 | 5,144 | 6,321 | 162 | 6,160 |
| **Department of Defense-Military Programs:** | | | | | | | | | |
| Military Personnel: | | | | | | | | | |
| Department of the Army | 7,223 | ...... | 7,223 | 43,918 | ...... | 43,918 | 45,987 | ...... | 45,987 |
| Department of the Navy | 5,351 | ...... | 5,351 | 32,611 | ...... | 32,611 | 31,753 | ...... | 31,753 |
| Department of the Air Force | 3,726 | ...... | 3,726 | 24,786 | ...... | 24,786 | 24,792 | ...... | 24,792 |
| Defense Agencies | ...... | ...... | ...... | 6,337 | ...... | 6,337 | 6,791 | ...... | 6,791 |
| Total--Military Personnel | 16,299 | ...... | 16,299 | 107,652 | ...... | 107,652 | 109,324 | ...... | 109,324 |
| Operation and Maintenance: | | | | | | | | | |
| Department of the Army | 5,945 | ...... | 5,945 | 47,368 | ...... | 47,368 | 58,091 | ...... | 58,091 |
| Department of the Navy | 4,367 | ...... | 4,367 | 34,913 | ...... | 34,913 | 36,553 | ...... | 36,553 |
| Department of the Air Force | 4,171 | ...... | 4,171 | 33,171 | ...... | 33,171 | 35,467 | ...... | 35,467 |
| Defense Agencies | 6,548 | ...... | 6,548 | 44,384 | ...... | 44,384 | 45,365 | ...... | 45,365 |
| Total--Operation and Maintenance | 21,030 | ...... | 21,030 | 159,835 | ...... | 159,835 | 175,476 | ...... | 175,476 |
| International Reconstruction and Other Assistance: | | | | | | | | | |
| Department of the Army | (**) | ...... | (**) | 1 | ...... | 1 | 1 | ...... | 1 |
| Procurement: | | | | | | | | | |
| Department of the Army | 1,647 | ...... | 1,647 | 15,439 | ...... | 15,439 | 19,395 | ...... | 19,395 |
| Department of the Navy | 3,211 | ...... | 3,211 | 28,167 | ...... | 28,167 | 27,230 | ...... | 27,230 |
| Department of the Air Force | 1,576 | ...... | 1,576 | 25,046 | ...... | 25,046 | 24,957 | ...... | 24,957 |
| Defense Agencies | 596 | ...... | 596 | 4,535 | ...... | 4,535 | 4,570 | ...... | 4,570 |
| Total--Procurement | 7,029 | ...... | 7,029 | 73,186 | ...... | 73,186 | 76,153 | ...... | 76,153 |
| Research, Development, Test, and Evaluation: | | | | | | | | | |
| Department of the Army | 685 | ...... | 685 | 5,151 | ...... | 5,151 | 5,679 | ...... | 5,679 |
| Department of the Navy | 1,367 | ...... | 1,367 | 10,132 | ...... | 10,132 | 10,359 | ...... | 10,359 |
| Department of the Air Force | 1,230 | ...... | 1,230 | 14,646 | ...... | 14,646 | 16,158 | ...... | 16,158 |
| Defense Agencies | 1,396 | ...... | 1,396 | 11,895 | ...... | 11,895 | 11,996 | ...... | 11,996 |
| Total--Research, Development, Test, and Evaluation | 4,678 | ...... | 4,678 | 41,825 | ...... | 41,825 | 44,192 | ...... | 44,192 |
| Military Construction: | | | | | | | | | |
| Department of the Army | 301 | ...... | 301 | 1,937 | ...... | 1,937 | 2,773 | ...... | 2,773 |
| Department of the Navy | 142 | ...... | 142 | 1,339 | ...... | 1,339 | 1,767 | ...... | 1,767 |
| Department of the Air Force | 99 | ...... | 99 | 794 | ...... | 794 | 950 | ...... | 950 |
| Defense Agencies | 190 | ...... | 190 | 2,291 | ...... | 2,291 | 2,617 | ...... | 2,617 |
| Total--Military Construction | 732 | ...... | 732 | 6,362 | ...... | 6,362 | 8,107 | ...... | 8,107 |
| Family Housing: | | | | | | | | | |
| Department of the Army | 331 | ...... | 331 | 289 | ...... | 289 | 406 | ...... | 406 |
| Department of the Navy | 33 | ...... | 33 | 234 | ...... | 234 | 270 | ...... | 270 |
| Department of the Air Force | 34 | ...... | 34 | 264 | ...... | 264 | 433 | ...... | 433 |
| Defense Agencies | 6 | 8 | -2 | 60 | 18 | 42 | 317 | 77 | 240 |
| Revolving and Management Funds: | | | | | | | | | |
| Department of the Navy | -59 | ...... | -59 | 745 | ...... | 745 | 749 | ...... | 749 |
| Defense Agencies: | | | | | | | | | |
| Working Capital Fund | -544 | ...... | -544 | 1,150 | ...... | 1,150 | 1,321 | ...... | 1,321 |
| Other | 78 | ...... | 78 | 156 | ...... | 156 | 213 | ...... | 213 |
| Allowances | 7 | ...... | 7 | 47 | ...... | 47 | -34 | ...... | -34 |
| Trust Funds: | | | | | | | | | |
| Department of the Army | 1 | ...... | 1 | 6 | ...... | 6 | 6 | ...... | 6 |
| Department of the Navy | 1 | ...... | 1 | 15 | ...... | 15 | 15 | ...... | 15 |
| Department of the Air Force | (**) | (**) | (**) | 2 | (**) | 1 | 2 | ...... | 2 |
| Defense Agencies | 14 | ...... | 14 | 158 | ...... | 158 | 238 | ...... | 238 |
| Proprietary Receipts from the Public: | | | | | | | | | |
| Department of the Army | ...... | 567 | -567 | ...... | 895 | -895 | ...... | 921 | -921 |
| Department of the Navy | ...... | 12 | -12 | ...... | 87 | -87 | ...... | 78 | -78 |
| Department of the Air Force | ...... | 19 | -19 | ...... | 13 | -13 | ...... | 21 | -21 |
| Defense Agencies | ...... | 177 | -177 | ...... | 861 | -861 | ...... | 577 | -577 |
| Intrabudgetary Transactions: | | | | | | | | | |
| Department of the Army | -10 | ...... | -10 | -24 | ...... | -24 | -324 | ...... | -324 |
| Department of the Navy | -147 | ...... | -147 | -153 | ...... | -153 | 149 | ...... | 149 |
| Department of the Air Force | 63 | ...... | 63 | 71 | ...... | 71 | 15 | ...... | 15 |
| Defense Agencies | 98 | ...... | 98 | 294 | ...... | 294 | 35 | ...... | 35 |
| Offsetting Governmental Receipts: | | | | | | | | | |
| Department of the Army | ...... | (**) | (**) | ...... | 1 | -1 | ...... | (**) | (**) |
| **Total--Department of Defense--Military Programs** | 49,674 | 783 | 48,891 | 392,175 | 1,874 | 390,300 | 417,063 | 1,674 | 415,390 |

[$ millions]

| Classification | This Month | | | Current Fiscal Year to Date | | | Prior Fiscal Year to Date | | |
|---|---|---|---|---|---|---|---|---|---|
| | Gross Outlays | Applicable Receipts | Outlays | Gross Outlays | Applicable Receipts | Outlays | Gross Outlays | Applicable Receipts | Outlays |
| **Department of Education:** | | | | | | | | | |
| Office of Elementary and Secondary Education: | | | | | | | | | |
| Accelerating Achievement and Ensuring Equity | 1,609 | ...... | 1,609 | 10,762 | ...... | 10,762 | 11,434 | ...... | 11,434 |
| Impact Aid | 93 | ...... | 93 | 1,043 | ...... | 1,043 | 1,316 | ...... | 1,316 |
| Education Improvement Programs | 348 | ...... | 348 | 2,898 | ...... | 2,898 | 3,104 | ...... | 3,104 |
| State Fiscal Stabilization Fund, Recovery Act | 125 | ...... | 125 | 950 | ...... | 950 | 768 | ...... | 768 |
| Other | 33 | ...... | 33 | 249 | ...... | 249 | 504 | ...... | 504 |
| Total--Office of Elementary and Secondary Education | 2,209 | ...... | 2,209 | 15,901 | ...... | 15,901 | 17,127 | ...... | 17,127 |
| Office of Innovation and Improvement | 83 | ...... | 83 | 750 | ...... | 750 | 676 | ...... | 676 |
| Office of English Language Acquisition | 51 | ...... | 51 | 484 | ...... | 484 | 456 | ...... | 456 |
| Office of Special Education and Rehabilitative Services: | | | | | | | | | |
| Special Education | 1,201 | ...... | 1,201 | 8,648 | ...... | 8,648 | 8,614 | ...... | 8,614 |
| Rehabilitation Services and Disability Research | 274 | ...... | 274 | 2,227 | ...... | 2,227 | 2,350 | ...... | 2,350 |
| Special Institutions for Persons with Disabilities | 19 | ...... | 19 | 145 | ...... | 145 | 140 | ...... | 140 |
| Office of Vocational and Adult Education | 143 | ...... | 143 | 1,082 | ...... | 1,082 | 1,157 | ...... | 1,157 |
| Office of Postsecondary Education: | | | | | | | | | |
| Higher Education | 177 | ...... | 177 | 1,423 | ...... | 1,423 | 1,525 | ...... | 1,525 |
| Other | -1 | 1 | -2 | 172 | 9 | 163 | 170 | 13 | 158 |
| Total--Office of Postsecondary Education | 176 | 1 | 174 | 1,595 | 9 | 1,586 | 1,695 | 13 | 1,683 |
| Office of Federal Student Aid: | | | | | | | | | |
| Student Financial Assistance | 911 | ...... | 911 | 21,328 | ...... | 21,328 | 22,217 | ...... | 22,217 |
| Student Aid Administration | 107 | ...... | 107 | 852 | ...... | 852 | 876 | ...... | 876 |
| Federal Student Loan Reserve Fund | ...... | ...... | ...... | 166 | ...... | 166 | 179 | ...... | 179 |
| Federal Direct Student Loans | ...... | ...... | ...... | (**) | ...... | (**) | (**) | ...... | (**) |
| Federal Family Education Loans | -26 | ...... | -26 | -183 | ...... | -183 | -288 | ...... | -288 |
| Other | (**) | ...... | (**) | 8 | ...... | 8 | 8 | ...... | 8 |
| Total--Office of Federal Student Aid | 991 | ...... | 991 | 22,172 | ...... | 22,172 | 22,992 | ...... | 22,992 |
| Institute of Education Sciences | 56 | ...... | 56 | 418 | ...... | 418 | 515 | ...... | 515 |
| Departmental Management | 47 | ...... | 47 | 385 | ...... | 385 | 398 | ...... | 398 |
| Other | (**) | ...... | (**) | 1 | ...... | 1 | 5 | ...... | 5 |
| Proprietary Receipts from the Public | ...... | 149 | -149 | ...... | 17,839 | -17,839 | ...... | 19,758 | -19,758 |
| Intrabudgetary Transactions | 64 | ...... | 64 | 41 | ...... | 41 | -60 | ...... | -60 |
| **Total--Department of Education** | 5,315 | 150 | 5,164 | 53,849 | 17,848 | 36,000 | 56,064 | 19,771 | 36,294 |
| **Department of Energy:** | | | | | | | | | |
| National Nuclear Security Administration: | | | | | | | | | |
| Naval Reactors | 86 | ...... | 86 | 710 | ...... | 710 | 613 | ...... | 613 |
| Weapons Activities | 552 | ...... | 552 | 5,076 | ...... | 5,076 | 4,769 | ...... | 4,769 |
| Defense Nuclear Nonproliferation | 110 | ...... | 110 | 1,238 | ...... | 1,238 | 1,469 | ...... | 1,469 |
| Other | 46 | ...... | 46 | 245 | ...... | 245 | 278 | ...... | 278 |
| Environmental and Other Defense Activities: | | | | | | | | | |
| Defense Environmental Cleanup | 379 | ...... | 379 | 3,116 | ...... | 3,116 | 3,271 | ...... | 3,271 |
| Other Defense Activities | 65 | ...... | 65 | 474 | ...... | 474 | 542 | ...... | 542 |
| Defense Nuclear Waste Disposal | (**) | ...... | (**) | 2 | ...... | 2 | 4 | ...... | 4 |
| Energy Programs: | | | | | | | | | |
| Science | 402 | ...... | 402 | 3,297 | ...... | 3,297 | 3,427 | ...... | 3,427 |
| Energy Supply | 124 | ...... | 124 | 949 | ...... | 949 | 1,271 | ...... | 1,271 |
| Energy Efficiency and Renewable Energy | 178 | ...... | 178 | 1,389 | ...... | 1,389 | 2,132 | ...... | 2,132 |
| Fossil Energy Research and Development | 80 | ...... | 80 | 558 | ...... | 558 | 615 | ...... | 615 |
| Uranium Enrichment Decontamination and Decommissioning Fund | 36 | ...... | 36 | 264 | ...... | 264 | 263 | ...... | 263 |
| Advanced Technology Vehicles Manufacturing Loan Program | (**) | ...... | (**) | 17 | ...... | 17 | 119 | ...... | 119 |
| Title 17 Innovative Technology Loan Guarantee Program | 6 | ...... | 6 | 167 | ...... | 167 | 404 | ...... | 404 |
| Other | 82 | 7 | 75 | 615 | 47 | 569 | 620 | 37 | 583 |
| Total--Energy Programs | 908 | 7 | 901 | 7,256 | 47 | 7,209 | 8,851 | 37 | 8,814 |
| Power Marketing Administration | 311 | 350 | -38 | 2,484 | 2,644 | -160 | 2,428 | 2,801 | -373 |
| Departmental Administration | 12 | ...... | 12 | 95 | ...... | 95 | 179 | ...... | 179 |
| Proprietary Receipts from the Public | ...... | 253 | -253 | ...... | 1,439 | -1,439 | ...... | 2,085 | -2,085 |
| Intrabudgetary Transactions | -151 | ...... | -151 | -1,024 | ...... | -1,024 | -1,031 | ...... | -1,031 |
| **Total--Department of Energy** | 2,320 | 610 | 1,710 | 19,672 | 4,129 | 15,543 | 21,372 | 4,922 | 16,449 |

# Table 5. Outlays of the U.S. Government, May 2014 and Other Periods —Continued

[$ millions]

| Classification | This Month Gross Outlays | This Month Applicable Receipts | This Month Outlays | Current Fiscal Year to Date Gross Outlays | Current Fiscal Year to Date Applicable Receipts | Current Fiscal Year to Date Outlays | Prior Fiscal Year to Date Gross Outlays | Prior Fiscal Year to Date Applicable Receipts | Prior Fiscal Year to Date Outlays |
|---|---|---|---|---|---|---|---|---|---|
| **Department of Health and Human Services:** | | | | | | | | | |
| Food and Drug Administration | 260 | 1 | 260 | 1,472 | 5 | 1,467 | 1,200 | 6 | 1,194 |
| Health Resources and Services Administration | 714 | 1 | 714 | 6,004 | 5 | 5,999 | 5,597 | 5 | 5,592 |
| Indian Health Services | 221 | ...... | 221 | 3,745 | ...... | 3,745 | 2,803 | ...... | 2,803 |
| Centers for Disease Control and Prevention | 446 | ...... | 446 | 4,076 | ...... | 4,076 | 4,212 | ...... | 4,212 |
| National Institutes of Health | 2,471 | ...... | 2,471 | 19,884 | ...... | 19,884 | 20,495 | ...... | 20,495 |
| Substance Abuse and Mental Health Services Administration | 267 | ...... | 267 | 2,155 | ...... | 2,155 | 2,190 | ...... | 2,190 |
| Agency for Healthcare Research and Quality | -4 | ...... | -4 | 49 | ...... | 49 | 300 | ...... | 300 |
| Centers for Medicare and Medicaid Services: | | | | | | | | | |
| Grants to States for Medicaid | 25,709 | ...... | 25,709 | 190,950 | ...... | 190,950 | 176,575 | ...... | 176,575 |
| Payments to Health Care Trust Funds | 23,972 | ...... | 23,972 | 180,736 | ...... | 180,736 | 161,348 | ...... | 161,348 |
| Children's Health Insurance Fund | 632 | ...... | 632 | 6,905 | ...... | 6,905 | 6,040 | ...... | 6,040 |
| State Grants and Demonstrations | 40 | ...... | 40 | 325 | ...... | 325 | 373 | ...... | 373 |
| Federal Hospital Insurance Trust Fund: | | | | | | | | | |
| Benefit Payments | 29,185 | ...... | 29,185 | 177,518 | ...... | 177,518 | 179,549 | ...... | 179,549 |
| Administrative Expenses | 370 | ...... | 370 | 5,751 | ...... | 5,751 | 4,950 | ...... | 4,950 |
| Total--FHI Trust Fund | 29,555 | ...... | 29,555 | 183,269 | ...... | 183,269 | 184,499 | ...... | 184,499 |
| Health Care Fraud and Abuse Control | 100 | ...... | 100 | 839 | ...... | 839 | 947 | ...... | 947 |
| Federal Supplementary Medical Insurance Trust Fund: | | | | | | | | | |
| Benefit Payments | 29,242 | ...... | 29,242 | 171,363 | ...... | 171,363 | 164,441 | ...... | 164,441 |
| Administrative Expenses | 716 | ...... | 716 | 4,305 | ...... | 4,305 | 4,403 | ...... | 4,403 |
| Medicare Prescription Drugs: | | | | | | | | | |
| Benefit Payments | 10,123 | ...... | 10,123 | 47,692 | ...... | 47,692 | 45,393 | ...... | 45,393 |
| Administrative Expenses | 30 | ...... | 30 | 271 | ...... | 271 | 255 | ...... | 255 |
| Total--FSMI Trust Fund | 40,110 | ...... | 40,110 | 223,631 | ...... | 223,631 | 214,492 | ...... | 214,492 |
| Other | 284 | ...... | 284 | 2,551 | (**) | 2,551 | 3,015 | ...... | 3,015 |
| Total--Centers for Medicare and Medicaid Services | 120,402 | ...... | 120,402 | 789,206 | ...... | 789,206 | 747,290 | ...... | 747,290 |
| Administration for Children and Families | | | | | | | | | |
| Temporary Assistance for Needy Families | 1,286 | ...... | 1,286 | 10,497 | ...... | 10,497 | 11,194 | ...... | 11,194 |
| Contingency Fund | 114 | ...... | 114 | 436 | ...... | 436 | 565 | ...... | 565 |
| Payments to States for Child Support Enforcement | | | | | | | | | |
| and Family Support Programs | 256 | ...... | 256 | 2,200 | ...... | 2,200 | 2,156 | ...... | 2,156 |
| Low Income Home Energy Assistance | 223 | ...... | 223 | 2,886 | ...... | 2,886 | 2,825 | ...... | 2,825 |
| Refugee and Entrant Assistance | 110 | ...... | 110 | 701 | ...... | 701 | 621 | ...... | 621 |
| Child Care Entitlement to States | 252 | ...... | 252 | 1,815 | ...... | 1,815 | 2,110 | ...... | 2,110 |
| Payments to States for the Child Care | | | | | | | | | |
| and Development Block Grant | 195 | ...... | 195 | 1,414 | ...... | 1,414 | 1,176 | ...... | 1,176 |
| Social Services Block Grant | 113 | ...... | 113 | 1,100 | ...... | 1,100 | 1,289 | ...... | 1,289 |
| Children and Families Services Programs | 836 | ...... | 836 | 6,368 | ...... | 6,368 | 6,790 | ...... | 6,790 |
| Payments to States for Foster Care and Adoption Assistance | 550 | ...... | 550 | 4,676 | ...... | 4,676 | 4,484 | ...... | 4,484 |
| Other | 47 | ...... | 47 | 362 | ...... | 362 | 394 | ...... | 394 |
| Total--Administration for Children and Families | 3,981 | ...... | 3,981 | 32,454 | ...... | 32,454 | 33,603 | ...... | 33,603 |
| Administration on Aging | 136 | ...... | 136 | 954 | ...... | 954 | 985 | ...... | 985 |
| Departmental Management | 386 | ...... | 386 | 1,862 | ...... | 1,862 | 2,143 | ...... | 2,143 |
| Other | 106 | ...... | 106 | 524 | ...... | 524 | 416 | ...... | 416 |
| Proprietary Receipts from the Public | ...... | 9,871 | -9,871 | ...... | 58,587 | -58,587 | ...... | 53,334 | -53,334 |
| Intrabudgetary Transactions: | | | | | | | | | |
| Payments for Health Insurance for the Aged: | | | | | | | | | |
| Federal Supplementary Medical Insurance Trust Fund | -23,965 | ...... | -23,965 | -167,696 | ...... | -167,696 | -152,251 | ...... | -152,251 |
| Payments for Tax and Other Credits: | | | | | | | | | |
| Federal Hospital Insurance Trust Fund | -7 | ...... | -7 | -13,037 | ...... | -13,037 | -9,070 | ...... | -9,070 |
| Other | -109 | ...... | -109 | 934 | ...... | 934 | -135 | ...... | -135 |
| Total--Department of Health and Human Services | 105,305 | 9,873 | 95,432 | 682,587 | 58,597 | 623,990 | 659,779 | 53,346 | 606,433 |
| **Department of Homeland Security:** | | | | | | | | | |
| Departmental Management and Operations | 77 | ...... | 77 | 646 | ...... | 646 | 813 | ...... | 813 |
| Citizenship and Immigration Services | 259 | ...... | 259 | 1,907 | ...... | 1,907 | 1,871 | ...... | 1,871 |
| United States Secret Service | 142 | ...... | 142 | 1,164 | ...... | 1,164 | 1,232 | ...... | 1,232 |
| Transportation Security Administration | 379 | ...... | 379 | 3,472 | ...... | 3,472 | 3,818 | ...... | 3,818 |
| Immigration and Customs Enforcement | 422 | ...... | 422 | 3,500 | ...... | 3,500 | 3,814 | ...... | 3,814 |
| Customs and Border Protection | 912 | -1 | 912 | 7,598 | (**) | 7,598 | 8,077 | ...... | 8,077 |
| United States Coast Guard | 1,000 | ...... | 1,000 | 7,063 | ...... | 7,063 | 7,092 | 3 | 7,089 |
| National Protection and Programs Directorate | 103 | ...... | 103 | 833 | ...... | 833 | 933 | ...... | 933 |
| Federal Emergency Management Agency: | | | | | | | | | |
| State and Local Programs | 241 | ...... | 241 | 1,736 | ...... | 1,736 | 2,360 | ...... | 2,360 |
| Firefighter Assistance Grants | 50 | ...... | 50 | 424 | ...... | 424 | 482 | ...... | 482 |
| Disaster Relief | 483 | ...... | 483 | 3,747 | ...... | 3,747 | 6,931 | ...... | 6,931 |
| National Flood Insurance Fund | 71 | 224 | -153 | 678 | 1,461 | -784 | 8,128 | 990 | 7,138 |
| Other | 88 | ...... | 88 | 835 | ...... | 835 | 865 | ...... | 865 |
| Total--Federal Emergency Management Agency | 933 | 224 | 709 | 7,420 | 1,461 | 5,959 | 18,767 | 990 | 17,777 |
| Science and Technology | 83 | ...... | 83 | 456 | ...... | 456 | 374 | ...... | 374 |
| Domestic Nuclear Detection Office | 34 | ...... | 34 | 198 | ...... | 198 | 186 | ...... | 186 |
| Other | 30 | ...... | 30 | 251 | ...... | 251 | 300 | ...... | 300 |
| Proprietary Receipts from the Public | ...... | 15 | -15 | ...... | 159 | -159 | ...... | 186 | -186 |
| Intrabudgetary Transactions | -61 | ...... | -61 | -6 | ...... | -6 | 17 | ...... | 17 |
| Offsetting Governmental Receipts | ...... | 999 | -999 | ...... | 5,083 | -5,083 | ...... | 4,910 | -4,910 |
| Total--Department of Homeland Security | 4,312 | 1,238 | 3,074 | 34,501 | 6,703 | 27,798 | 47,294 | 6,088 | 41,206 |

# Table 5. Outlays of the U.S. Government, May 2014 and Other Periods —Continued

[$ millions]

| Classification | This Month Gross Outlays | This Month Applicable Receipts | This Month Outlays | Current Fiscal Year to Date Gross Outlays | Current Fiscal Year to Date Applicable Receipts | Current Fiscal Year to Date Outlays | Prior Fiscal Year to Date Gross Outlays | Prior Fiscal Year to Date Applicable Receipts | Prior Fiscal Year to Date Outlays |
|---|---|---|---|---|---|---|---|---|---|
| **Department of Housing and Urban Development:** | | | | | | | | | |
| Public and Indian Housing Programs: | | | | | | | | | |
| Tenant Based Rental Assistance | 1,573 | ...... | 1,573 | 12,450 | ...... | 12,450 | 12,157 | ...... | 12,157 |
| Housing Certificate Fund | 27 | ...... | 27 | 239 | ...... | 239 | 340 | ...... | 340 |
| Project-Based Rental Assistance | 825 | ...... | 825 | 6,503 | ...... | 6,503 | 6,242 | ...... | 6,242 |
| Public Housing Capital Fund | 145 | ...... | 145 | 1,293 | ...... | 1,293 | 1,441 | ...... | 1,441 |
| Public Housing Operating Fund | 346 | ...... | 346 | 2,815 | ...... | 2,815 | 2,739 | ...... | 2,739 |
| Revitalization of Severely Distressed Public Housing (Hope VI) | 4 | ...... | 4 | 65 | ...... | 65 | 101 | ...... | 101 |
| Native American Housing Block Grant | 138 | ...... | 138 | 523 | ...... | 523 | 346 | ...... | 346 |
| Other | 1 | ...... | 1 | 40 | ...... | 40 | 5 | ...... | 5 |
| Total--Public and Indian Housing Programs | 3,058 | ...... | 3,058 | 23,929 | ...... | 23,929 | 23,372 | ...... | 23,372 |
| Community Planning and Development: | | | | | | | | | |
| Housing Opportunities for Persons with AIDS | 22 | ...... | 22 | 194 | ...... | 194 | 200 | ...... | 200 |
| Community Development Fund | 463 | ...... | 463 | 4,293 | ...... | 4,293 | 3,912 | ...... | 3,912 |
| Home Investment Partnership Program | 95 | ...... | 95 | 827 | ...... | 827 | 964 | ...... | 964 |
| Neighborhood Stabilization Program | 13 | ...... | 13 | 264 | ...... | 264 | 658 | ...... | 658 |
| Homeless Assistance Grants | 155 | ...... | 155 | 1,267 | ...... | 1,267 | 1,165 | ...... | 1,165 |
| Other | 8 | ...... | 8 | 63 | (**) | 63 | 64 | ...... | 64 |
| Total--Community Planning and Development | 755 | ...... | 755 | 6,908 | (**) | 6,908 | 6,963 | ...... | 6,963 |
| Housing Programs: | | | | | | | | | |
| Credit Accounts: | | | | | | | | | |
| FHA-Mutual Mortgage Insurance Fund, Program Account | 9 | ...... | 9 | 5,836 | ...... | 5,836 | 70 | ...... | 70 |
| FHA-Mutual Mortgage Insurance Capital Reserve Account | -1,096 | ...... | -1,096 | -9,778 | ...... | -9,778 | -10,545 | ...... | -10,545 |
| FHA-Mutual Mortgage and Cooperative Housing Insurance Fund, Liquidating Account | -1 | 1 | -2 | 16 | 12 | 4 | 24 | 13 | 11 |
| FHA-General and Special Risk Fund, Program Account | 210 | ...... | 210 | 210 | ...... | 210 | (**) | ...... | (**) |
| FHA-General and Special Risk Fund, Liquidating Account | 5 | 15 | -10 | 38 | 159 | -121 | 57 | 164 | -106 |
| Housing for the Elderly or Handicapped Fund, Liquidating Account | (**) | 46 | -46 | (**) | 321 | -321 | 1 | 411 | -410 |
| Housing for the Elderly | 74 | ...... | 74 | 594 | ...... | 594 | 575 | ...... | 575 |
| Housing for Persons with Disabilities | 18 | ...... | 18 | 153 | ...... | 153 | 141 | ...... | 141 |
| Other Assisted Housing Programs | 25 | ...... | 25 | 222 | ...... | 222 | 268 | ...... | 268 |
| Other | 3 | 7 | -4 | 52 | 31 | 21 | 79 | 24 | 55 |
| Total--Housing Programs | -753 | 69 | -822 | -2,656 | 523 | -3,179 | -9,329 | 612 | -9,941 |
| Government National Mortgage Association: | | | | | | | | | |
| Guarantees of Mortgage-Backed Securities | 5 | (**) | 5 | 20 | 51 | -30 | 91 | 35 | 55 |
| Management and Administration | 136 | ...... | 136 | 1,141 | ...... | 1,141 | 1,209 | ...... | 1,209 |
| Other | 17 | ...... | 17 | 132 | ...... | 132 | 172 | ...... | 172 |
| Proprietary Receipts from the Public: | | | | | | | | | |
| FHA-General and Special Risk Fund | ...... | 2,115 | -2,115 | ...... | 2,464 | -2,464 | ...... | 469 | -469 |
| Other | ...... | -10 | 10 | ...... | 17 | -17 | ...... | -1 | 1 |
| Intrabudgetary Transactions | -3 | ...... | -3 | -8 | ...... | -8 | -21 | ...... | -21 |
| Offsetting Governmental Receipts | ...... | (**) | (**) | ...... | 2 | -2 | ...... | 2 | -2 |
| **Total--Department of Housing and Urban Development** | 3,217 | 2,175 | 1,042 | 29,467 | 3,057 | 26,410 | 22,457 | 1,118 | 21,339 |
| **Department of the Interior:** | | | | | | | | | |
| Land and Minerals Management: | | | | | | | | | |
| Bureau of Land Management: | | | | | | | | | |
| Management of Lands and Resources | 97 | ...... | 97 | 638 | ...... | 638 | 623 | ...... | 623 |
| Other | 39 | 14 | 24 | 310 | -94 | 404 | 371 | 117 | 254 |
| Bureau of Ocean Energy Management, Regulation and Enforcement | 5 | ...... | 5 | 30 | ...... | 30 | -17 | ...... | -17 |
| Office of Surface Mining Reclamation and Enforcement | 31 | ...... | 31 | 407 | ...... | 407 | 523 | ...... | 523 |
| Total--Land and Minerals Management | 172 | 14 | 158 | 1,386 | -94 | 1,479 | 1,499 | 117 | 1,382 |
| Water and Science: | | | | | | | | | |
| Bureau of Reclamation: | | | | | | | | | |
| Water and Related Resources | 44 | ...... | 44 | 521 | ...... | 521 | 529 | ...... | 529 |
| Other | 59 | 37 | 22 | 869 | 290 | 579 | 453 | 241 | 212 |
| United States Geological Survey | 85 | ...... | 85 | 727 | ...... | 727 | 711 | ...... | 711 |
| Other | 1 | ...... | 1 | 10 | ...... | 10 | 16 | ...... | 16 |
| Total--Water and Science | 189 | 37 | 152 | 2,127 | 290 | 1,837 | 1,708 | 241 | 1,467 |
| Fish and Wildlife and Parks: | | | | | | | | | |
| United States Fish and Wildlife Service | 205 | ...... | 205 | 1,759 | ...... | 1,759 | 1,733 | ...... | 1,733 |
| National Park Service | 247 | ...... | 247 | 1,798 | ...... | 1,798 | 1,913 | ...... | 1,913 |
| Total--Fish and Wildlife and Parks | 452 | ...... | 452 | 3,557 | ...... | 3,557 | 3,646 | ...... | 3,646 |
| Bureau of Indian Affairs and Bureau of Indian Education | 307 | (**) | 307 | 1,650 | (**) | 1,650 | 1,174 | 1 | 1,173 |
| Departmental Offices: | | | | | | | | | |
| Mineral Leasing and Associated Payments | 194 | ...... | 194 | 1,423 | ...... | 1,423 | 1,221 | ...... | 1,221 |
| Other | 19 | ...... | 19 | 209 | ...... | 209 | 198 | ...... | 198 |
| Insular Affairs | 16 | ...... | 16 | 271 | ...... | 271 | 285 | ...... | 285 |
| Office of the Special Trustee for American Indians | 16 | ...... | 16 | 117 | ...... | 117 | 436 | ...... | 436 |
| Department-Wide Programs | 28 | ...... | 28 | 440 | ...... | 440 | 736 | ...... | 736 |
| Other | 13 | ...... | 13 | 111 | ...... | 111 | 130 | ...... | 130 |
| Proprietary Receipts from the Public | ...... | 535 | -535 | ...... | 3,786 | -3,786 | ...... | 3,532 | -3,532 |
| Intrabudgetary Transactions | -32 | ...... | -32 | -116 | ...... | -116 | -2,026 | ...... | -2,026 |
| **Total--Department of the Interior** | 1,375 | 587 | 788 | 11,175 | 3,982 | 7,193 | 9,007 | 3,890 | 5,117 |

## Table 5. Outlays of the U.S. Government, May 2014 and Other Periods —Continued
[$ millions]

| Classification | This Month | | | Current Fiscal Year to Date | | | Prior Fiscal Year to Date | | |
|---|---|---|---|---|---|---|---|---|---|
| | Gross Outlays | Applicable Receipts | Outlays | Gross Outlays | Applicable Receipts | Outlays | Gross Outlays | Applicable Receipts | Outlays |
| **Department of Justice:** | | | | | | | | | |
| General Administration | 2 | ...... | 2 | 139 | ...... | 139 | 662 | ...... | 662 |
| Legal Activities and United States Marshals: | | | | | | | | | |
| General Legal Activities | 64 | ...... | 64 | 541 | ...... | 541 | 563 | ...... | 563 |
| United States Attorneys | 179 | ...... | 179 | 1,226 | ...... | 1,226 | 1,340 | ...... | 1,340 |
| United States Marshals Service | 111 | ...... | 111 | 736 | ...... | 736 | 1,609 | ...... | 1,609 |
| Assets Forfeiture Fund | 104 | ...... | 104 | 821 | ...... | 821 | 722 | ...... | 722 |
| Other | 143 | ...... | 143 | 1,246 | ...... | 1,246 | 333 | ...... | 333 |
| Federal Bureau of Investigation | 466 | ...... | 466 | 5,178 | ...... | 5,178 | 5,559 | ...... | 5,559 |
| Drug Enforcement Administration | 185 | ...... | 185 | 1,488 | ...... | 1,488 | 1,561 | ...... | 1,561 |
| Bureau of Alcohol, Tobacco, Firearms, and Explosives | 84 | ...... | 84 | 709 | ...... | 709 | 762 | ...... | 762 |
| Federal Prison System | 603 | 30 | 573 | 4,722 | 252 | 4,470 | 4,798 | 254 | 4,543 |
| Office of Justice Programs: | | | | | | | | | |
| State and Local Law Enforcement Assistance | 66 | ...... | 66 | 878 | ...... | 878 | 968 | ...... | 968 |
| Community Oriented Policing Services | 27 | ...... | 27 | 227 | ...... | 227 | 373 | ...... | 373 |
| Crime Victims Fund | 75 | ...... | 75 | 463 | ...... | 463 | 470 | ...... | 470 |
| Other | 88 | ...... | 88 | 639 | ...... | 639 | 687 | ...... | 687 |
| Other | 66 | ...... | 66 | 435 | ...... | 435 | 527 | ...... | 527 |
| Proprietary Receipts from the Public | ...... | -51 | 51 | ...... | 2,137 | -2,137 | ...... | 192 | -192 |
| Intrabudgetary Transactions | -259 | ...... | -259 | 453 | ...... | 453 | 311 | ...... | 311 |
| Offsetting Governmental Receipts | ...... | 50 | -50 | ...... | 351 | -351 | ...... | 370 | -370 |
| **Total--Department of Justice** | **2,004** | **29** | **1,975** | **19,899** | **2,741** | **17,158** | **21,244** | **815** | **20,429** |
| **Department of Labor:** | | | | | | | | | |
| Employment and Training Administration: | | | | | | | | | |
| Training and Employment Services | 250 | ...... | 250 | 2,023 | ...... | 2,023 | 2,351 | ...... | 2,351 |
| Office of Job Corps | 150 | ...... | 150 | 1,054 | ...... | 1,054 | 1,081 | ...... | 1,081 |
| Community Service Employment for Older Americans | 34 | ...... | 34 | 273 | ...... | 273 | 284 | ...... | 284 |
| Federal Unemployment Benefits and Allowances | 49 | ...... | 49 | 346 | ...... | 346 | 325 | ...... | 325 |
| Federal Additional Unemployment Compensation Program-Recovery Act | -1 | ...... | -1 | -8 | ...... | -8 | -14 | ...... | -14 |
| State Unemployment Insurance and Employment Service Operations | 87 | ...... | 87 | 226 | ...... | 226 | 85 | ...... | 85 |
| Payments to the Unemployment Trust Fund | ...... | ...... | ...... | 5,028 | ...... | 5,028 | 31,479 | ...... | 31,479 |
| Advances to the Unemployment Trust Fund and Other Funds | ...... | ...... | ...... | 10 | ...... | 10 | ...... | ...... | ...... |
| Program Administration | 18 | ...... | 18 | 64 | ...... | 64 | 64 | ...... | 64 |
| Unemployment Trust Fund: | | | | | | | | | |
| Federal-State Unemployment Insurance: | | | | | | | | | |
| State Unemployment Benefits | 2,892 | ...... | 2,892 | 31,678 | ...... | 31,678 | 48,465 | ...... | 48,465 |
| State Administrative Expenses | 228 | ...... | 228 | 2,508 | ...... | 2,508 | 2,907 | ...... | 2,907 |
| Federal Administrative Expenses | 17 | ...... | 17 | 335 | ...... | 335 | 290 | ...... | 290 |
| Other | 99 | ...... | 99 | 99 | ...... | 99 | 1 | ...... | 1 |
| **Total--Unemployment Trust Fund** | **3,235** | ...... | **3,235** | **34,620** | ...... | **34,620** | **51,662** | ...... | **51,662** |
| Other | 36 | ...... | 36 | 374 | ...... | 374 | 191 | ...... | 191 |
| **Total--Employment and Training Administration** | **3,859** | ...... | **3,859** | **44,011** | ...... | **44,011** | **87,508** | ...... | **87,508** |

# Table 5. Outlays of the U.S. Government, May 2014 and Other Periods —Continued

[$ millions]

| Classification | This Month Gross Outlays | This Month Applicable Receipts | This Month Outlays | Current Fiscal Year to Date Gross Outlays | Current Fiscal Year to Date Applicable Receipts | Current Fiscal Year to Date Outlays | Prior Fiscal Year to Date Gross Outlays | Prior Fiscal Year to Date Applicable Receipts | Prior Fiscal Year to Date Outlays |
|---|---|---|---|---|---|---|---|---|---|
| **Department of Labor:—Continued** | | | | | | | | | |
| Pension Benefit Guaranty Corporation | 500 | 551 | -50 | 3,985 | 3,662 | 324 | 3,922 | 4,454 | -532 |
| Employment Standards Administration | (**) | ...... | (**) | 1 | ...... | 1 | 6 | ...... | 6 |
| Office of Workers' Compensation Programs: | | | | | | | | | |
| Special Benefits | 250 | ...... | 250 | -833 | ...... | -833 | -703 | ...... | -703 |
| Energy Employees Occupational | | | | | | | | | |
| Illness Compensation Fund | 120 | ...... | 120 | 703 | ...... | 703 | 886 | ...... | 886 |
| Special Benefits for Disabled Coal Miners | 11 | ...... | 11 | 87 | ...... | 87 | 100 | ...... | 100 |
| Black Lung Disability Trust Fund | 18 | ...... | 18 | 149 | ...... | 149 | 158 | ...... | 158 |
| Other | 32 | ...... | 32 | 234 | ...... | 234 | 251 | ...... | 251 |
| Wage and Hour Division | 27 | ...... | 27 | 178 | ...... | 178 | 191 | ...... | 191 |
| Occupational Safety and Health Administration | 48 | ...... | 48 | 351 | ...... | 351 | 375 | ...... | 375 |
| Mine Safety and Health Administration | 39 | ...... | 39 | 234 | ...... | 234 | 242 | ...... | 242 |
| Bureau of Labor Statistics | 47 | ...... | 47 | 339 | ...... | 339 | 362 | ...... | 362 |
| Departmental Management | 23 | ...... | 23 | 254 | ...... | 254 | 350 | ...... | 350 |
| Other | 31 | ...... | 31 | 204 | ...... | 204 | 215 | ...... | 215 |
| Proprietary Receipts from the Public | ...... | 3 | -3 | ...... | 6 | -6 | ...... | 12 | -12 |
| Intrabudgetary Transactions | -74 | ...... | -74 | -5,762 | ...... | -5,762 | -32,142 | ...... | -32,142 |
| **Total--Department of Labor** | **4,930** | **554** | **4,376** | **44,138** | **3,668** | **40,470** | **61,720** | **4,466** | **57,254** |
| **Department of State:** | | | | | | | | | |
| Administration of Foreign Affairs: | | | | | | | | | |
| Diplomatic and Consular Programs | 947 | ...... | 947 | 5,425 | ...... | 5,425 | 5,606 | ...... | 5,606 |
| Educational and Cultural Exchange Programs | 56 | ...... | 56 | 380 | ...... | 380 | 413 | ...... | 413 |
| Embassy Security, Construction, and Maintenance | 26 | ...... | 26 | 1,126 | ...... | 1,126 | 1,411 | ...... | 1,411 |
| Payment to Foreign Service Retirement and | | | | | | | | | |
| Disability Fund | 79 | ...... | 79 | 159 | ...... | 159 | 159 | ...... | 159 |
| Foreign Service Retirement and Disability Fund | 76 | ...... | 76 | 611 | ...... | 611 | 595 | ...... | 595 |
| Other | -371 | ...... | -371 | 176 | ...... | 176 | 63 | ...... | 63 |
| Total--Administration of Foreign Affairs | 814 | ...... | 814 | 7,877 | ...... | 7,877 | 8,247 | ...... | 8,247 |
| International Organizations and Conferences | 92 | ...... | 92 | 1,544 | ...... | 1,544 | 1,272 | ...... | 1,272 |
| Global Health and Child Survival | 538 | ...... | 538 | 5,183 | ...... | 5,183 | 4,285 | ...... | 4,285 |
| Migration and Refugee Assistance | 300 | ...... | 300 | 1,846 | ...... | 1,846 | 1,229 | ...... | 1,229 |
| International Narcotics Control and Law Enforcement | 113 | ...... | 113 | 811 | ...... | 811 | 963 | ...... | 963 |
| Andean Counterdrug Programs | 2 | ...... | 2 | 22 | ...... | 22 | 50 | ...... | 50 |
| Other | 38 | ...... | 38 | 279 | ...... | 279 | 277 | ...... | 277 |
| Proprietary Receipts from the Public | ...... | 26 | -26 | ...... | 52 | -52 | ...... | 29 | -29 |
| Intrabudgetary Transactions | -222 | ...... | -222 | -313 | ...... | -313 | -206 | ...... | -206 |
| **Total--Department of State** | **1,675** | **26** | **1,650** | **17,248** | **52** | **17,196** | **16,117** | **29** | **16,088** |
| **Department of Transportation:** | | | | | | | | | |
| Office of the Secretary | 58 | ...... | 58 | 473 | ...... | 473 | 639 | ...... | 639 |
| Federal Aviation Administration: | | | | | | | | | |
| Operations | -149 | ...... | -149 | 1,763 | ...... | 1,763 | 3,253 | ...... | 3,253 |
| Airport and Airway Trust Fund: | | | | | | | | | |
| Grants-In-Aid for Airports | 147 | ...... | 147 | 2,044 | ...... | 2,044 | 2,214 | ...... | 2,214 |
| Facilities and Equipment | 116 | ...... | 116 | 1,751 | ...... | 1,751 | 1,766 | ...... | 1,766 |
| Research, Engineering, and Development | 5 | ...... | 5 | 83 | ...... | 83 | 95 | ...... | 95 |
| Trust Fund Share of FAA Operations | 800 | ...... | 800 | 4,600 | ...... | 4,600 | 3,168 | ...... | 3,168 |
| Total--Airport and Airway Trust Fund | 1,068 | ...... | 1,068 | 8,478 | ...... | 8,478 | 7,243 | ...... | 7,243 |
| Other | 12 | 60 | -48 | -67 | 175 | -243 | 49 | 128 | -79 |
| Total--Federal Aviation Administration | 931 | 60 | 871 | 10,174 | 175 | 9,999 | 10,544 | 128 | 10,416 |
| Federal Highway Administration. | | | | | | | | | |
| Highway Trust Fund: | | | | | | | | | |
| Federal-Aid Highways | 2,729 | ...... | 2,729 | 24,301 | ...... | 24,301 | 23,716 | ...... | 23,716 |
| Other | (**) | 3 | -2 | 6 | 3 | 3 | 15 | 9 | 6 |
| Highway Infrastructure Investment, Recovery Act | 5 | ...... | 5 | 125 | ...... | 125 | 740 | ...... | 740 |
| Other Programs | 40 | ...... | 40 | 12,321 | ...... | 12,321 | 6,887 | ...... | 6,887 |
| Total--Federal Highway Administration | 2,775 | 3 | 2,772 | 36,753 | 3 | 36,751 | 31,359 | 9 | 31,350 |
| Federal Motor Carrier Safety Administration | 23 | ...... | 23 | 335 | ...... | 335 | 366 | ...... | 366 |
| National Highway Traffic Safety Administration | 53 | ...... | 53 | 569 | ...... | 569 | 504 | ...... | 504 |
| Federal Railroad Administration: | | | | | | | | | |
| Operating Subsidy Grants to the National Railroad | | | | | | | | | |
| Passenger Corporation | ...... | ...... | ...... | 270 | ...... | 270 | 343 | ...... | 343 |
| Capital and Debt Service Grants to the | | | | | | | | | |
| National Railroad Passenger Corporation | (**) | ...... | (**) | 558 | ...... | 558 | 623 | ...... | 623 |
| Capital Assistance for High Speed Rail Corridors | | | | | | | | | |
| and Intercity Passenger Rail Service | 10 | ...... | 10 | 643 | ...... | 643 | 338 | ...... | 338 |
| Other | 19 | (**) | 19 | 300 | (**) | 300 | 412 | ...... | 412 |
| Total--Federal Railroad Administration | 29 | (**) | 29 | 1,771 | (**) | 1,771 | 1,716 | ...... | 1,716 |

# Table 5. Outlays of the U.S. Government, May 2014 and Other Periods —Continued

[$ millions]

| Classification | This Month Gross Outlays | This Month Applicable Receipts | This Month Outlays | Current Fiscal Year to Date Gross Outlays | Current Fiscal Year to Date Applicable Receipts | Current Fiscal Year to Date Outlays | Prior Fiscal Year to Date Gross Outlays | Prior Fiscal Year to Date Applicable Receipts | Prior Fiscal Year to Date Outlays |
|---|---|---|---|---|---|---|---|---|---|
| **Department of Transportation:—Continued** | | | | | | | | | |
| Federal Transit Administration: | | | | | | | | | |
| Formula Grants | 9 | ...... | 9 | 64 | ...... | 64 | 100 | ...... | 100 |
| Capital Investment Grants | 268 | ...... | 268 | 1,167 | ...... | 1,167 | 1,320 | ...... | 1,320 |
| Transit Formula Grants | 870 | ...... | 870 | 5,458 | ...... | 5,458 | 4,946 | ...... | 4,946 |
| Transit Capital Assistance, Recovery Act | 15 | ...... | 15 | 128 | ...... | 128 | 431 | ...... | 431 |
| Other | 70 | ...... | 70 | 492 | ...... | 492 | 418 | ...... | 418 |
| Total--Federal Transit Administration | 1,231 | ...... | 1,231 | 7,309 | ...... | 7,309 | 7,215 | ...... | 7,215 |
| Maritime Administration | 43 | 1 | 42 | 158 | 7 | 151 | 305 | 12 | 293 |
| Other | -5 | 2 | -7 | 249 | 18 | 231 | 305 | 18 | 288 |
| Proprietary Receipts from the Public | ...... | 13 | -13 | ...... | 43 | -43 | ...... | 47 | -47 |
| Intrabudgetary Transactions: | | | | | | | | | |
| Payment from the General Fund, Highway Trust Fund | ...... | ...... | ...... | -11,693 | ...... | -11,693 | -6,200 | ...... | -6,200 |
| Other | (**) | ...... | (**) | -1 | ...... | -1 | -1 | ...... | -1 |
| Offsetting Governmental Receipts | ...... | 84 | -84 | ...... | 86 | -86 | ...... | 6 | -6 |
| Total--Department of Transportation | 5,139 | 163 | 4,976 | 46,099 | 333 | 45,766 | 46,752 | 220 | 46,532 |
| **Department of the Treasury:** | | | | | | | | | |
| Departmental Offices: | | | | | | | | | |
| Exchange Stabilization Fund | ...... | -1 | 1 | ...... | 78 | -78 | ...... | 97 | -97 |
| Grants for Specified Energy Property in Lieu of Tax Credit | 415 | ...... | 415 | 2,215 | ...... | 2,215 | 4,310 | ...... | 4,310 |
| Housing and Economic Recovery Programs | (**) | ...... | (**) | 3 | ...... | 3 | 7 | ...... | 7 |
| Troubled Asset Relief Programs | 381 | ...... | 381 | 2,980 | ...... | 2,980 | 3,198 | ...... | 3,198 |
| Other | 108 | ...... | 108 | 1,416 | ...... | 1,416 | 1,298 | ...... | 1,298 |
| Bureau of the Fiscal Service: | | | | | | | | | |
| Financial Management Service: | | | | | | | | | |
| Payment to the Resolution Funding Corporation | ...... | ...... | ...... | 1,976 | ...... | 1,976 | 1,976 | ...... | 1,976 |
| Financial Agent Services | 65 | ...... | 65 | 385 | ...... | 385 | 421 | ...... | 421 |
| Interest Paid to Credit Financing Accounts | ...... | ...... | ...... | 1 | ...... | 1 | (**) | ...... | (**) |
| Claims, Judgments, and Relief Acts | 113 | ...... | 113 | 1,282 | ...... | 1,282 | 5,021 | ...... | 5,021 |
| Other | 4 | 2 | 3 | 1,567 | 2 | 1,566 | 551 | (**) | 551 |
| Total--Financial Management Service | 182 | 2 | 180 | 5,212 | 2 | 5,210 | 7,970 | (**) | 7,970 |
| Bureau of the Public Debt | 27 | ...... | 27 | 351 | ...... | 351 | 153 | ...... | 153 |
| Total--Bureau of the Fiscal Service | 209 | 2 | 207 | 5,563 | 2 | 5,561 | 8,123 | (**) | 8,123 |
| Federal Financing Bank | -21 | ...... | -21 | -582 | ...... | -582 | -572 | ...... | -572 |
| Alcohol and Tobacco Tax and Trade Bureau: | | | | | | | | | |
| Salaries and Expenses | 8 | ...... | 8 | 62 | ...... | 62 | 64 | ...... | 64 |
| Internal Revenue Collections for Puerto Rico | 25 | ...... | 25 | 208 | ...... | 208 | 227 | ...... | 227 |
| Bureau of Engraving and Printing | -14 | ...... | -14 | -32 | ...... | -32 | 27 | ...... | 27 |
| United States Mint | 272 | 367 | -95 | 2,087 | 2,333 | -246 | 3,449 | 3,614 | -165 |
| Internal Revenue Service: | | | | | | | | | |
| Taxpayer Services | 179 | ...... | 179 | 1,539 | ...... | 1,539 | 1,666 | ...... | 1,666 |
| Enforcement | 376 | ...... | 376 | 3,199 | ...... | 3,199 | 3,516 | ...... | 3,516 |
| Operations Support | 310 | ...... | 310 | 2,725 | ...... | 2,725 | 2,699 | ...... | 2,699 |
| Build America Bond Payments, Recovery Act | 374 | ...... | 374 | 2,685 | ...... | 2,685 | 2,757 | ...... | 2,757 |
| Refundable Premium Tax Credits and Cost Sharing Reductions | 1,801 | ...... | 1,801 | 4,654 | ...... | 4,654 | ...... | ...... | ...... |
| Payment Where Earned Income Credit Exceeds Liability for Tax | 1,324 | ...... | 1,324 | 58,980 | ...... | 58,980 | 56,319 | ...... | 56,319 |
| Payment Where Child Tax Credit Exceeds Liability for Tax | 505 | ...... | 505 | 21,028 | ...... | 21,028 | 20,974 | ...... | 20,974 |
| Payment Where Tax Credits to Aid First Time Homebuyers Exceeds Liability for Tax | ...... | ...... | ...... | ...... | ...... | ...... | 13 | ...... | 13 |
| Payment Where Making Work Pay Credit Exceeds Liability for Tax, Recovery Act | -25 | ...... | -25 | -50 | ...... | -50 | -23 | ...... | -23 |
| Refunding Internal Revenue Collections, Interest | 102 | ...... | 102 | 679 | ...... | 679 | 2,293 | ...... | 2,293 |
| Other | 242 | ...... | 242 | 5,042 | 1 | 5,041 | 5,323 | 2 | 5,322 |
| Total--Internal Revenue Service | 5,188 | ...... | 5,188 | 100,481 | 1 | 100,480 | 95,536 | 2 | 95,535 |
| Comptroller of the Currency | 74 | 1 | 73 | 665 | 520 | 145 | 733 | 508 | 225 |
| Interest on the Public Debt: | | | | | | | | | |
| Interest on Treasury Debt Securities (Gross): | | | | | | | | | |
| Public Issues (Accrual Basis) | 26,476 | ...... | 26,476 | 167,090 | ...... | 167,090 | 166,252 | ...... | 166,252 |
| Special Issues (Cash Basis) | 5,605 | ...... | 5,605 | 88,964 | ...... | 88,964 | 85,978 | ...... | 85,978 |
| Total--Interest on Treasury Debt Securities (Gross) | 32,081 | ...... | 32,081 | 256,054 | ...... | 256,054 | 252,230 | ...... | 252,230 |
| Total--Interest on the Public Debt | 32,081 | ...... | 32,081 | 256,054 | ...... | 256,054 | 252,230 | ...... | 252,230 |
| Other | 6 | ...... | 6 | 58 | ...... | 58 | 67 | ...... | 67 |
| Proprietary Receipts from the Public | ...... | -403 | 403 | ...... | 66,357 | -66,357 | ...... | 28,802 | -28,802 |
| Intrabudgetary Transactions | -201 | ...... | -201 | -2,232 | ...... | -2,232 | -1,606 | ...... | -1,606 |
| Total--Department of the Treasury | 38,531 | -33 | 38,564 | 368,944 | 69,291 | 299,654 | 367,092 | 33,023 | 334,069 |

# Table 5. Outlays of the U.S. Government, May 2014 and Other Periods —Continued

[$ millions]

| Classification | This Month Gross Outlays | This Month Applicable Receipts | This Month Outlays | Current Fiscal Year to Date Gross Outlays | Current Fiscal Year to Date Applicable Receipts | Current Fiscal Year to Date Outlays | Prior Fiscal Year to Date Gross Outlays | Prior Fiscal Year to Date Applicable Receipts | Prior Fiscal Year to Date Outlays |
|---|---|---|---|---|---|---|---|---|---|
| **Department of Veterans Affairs:** | | | | | | | | | |
| Joint DOD-VA Medical Facility Demonstration Fund | 28 | ..... | 28 | 238 | ..... | 238 | 227 | ..... | 227 |
| Veterans Health Administration: | | | | | | | | | |
| Medical Services | 3,676 | ..... | 3,676 | 29,827 | ..... | 29,827 | 27,733 | ..... | 27,733 |
| Medical Support and Compliance | 430 | ..... | 430 | 3,740 | ..... | 3,740 | 3,511 | ..... | 3,511 |
| Medical Facilities | 377 | ..... | 377 | 3,448 | ..... | 3,448 | 3,582 | ..... | 3,582 |
| Other | 89 | 33 | 56 | 720 | 279 | 441 | 677 | 262 | 415 |
| Benefit Programs: | | | | | | | | | |
| Public Enterprise Funds: | | | | | | | | | |
| Housing Accounts | (**) | 2 | -1 | 3 | 14 | -11 | 4 | 15 | -11 |
| Other | 82 | 74 | 8 | 638 | 619 | 19 | 764 | 732 | 31 |
| Compensation and Pensions | 11,083 | ..... | 11,083 | 51,261 | ..... | 51,261 | 46,856 | ..... | 46,856 |
| Readjustment Benefits | 1,423 | ..... | 1,423 | 9,804 | ..... | 9,804 | 9,250 | ..... | 9,250 |
| Veterans Housing Benefit Program Fund | 43 | ..... | 43 | 2,118 | ..... | 2,118 | 45 | ..... | 45 |
| Insurance Funds: | | | | | | | | | |
| National Service Life | 82 | ..... | 82 | 644 | ..... | 644 | 689 | ..... | 689 |
| Veterans Special Life | 15 | 2 | 13 | 114 | 64 | 50 | 108 | 68 | 40 |
| Other | 2 | ..... | 2 | 47 | ..... | 47 | 40 | ..... | 40 |
| Total--Benefit Programs | 12,731 | 77 | 12,654 | 64,630 | 697 | 63,933 | 57,756 | 816 | 56,940 |
| Departmental Administration: | | | | | | | | | |
| Construction | 102 | ..... | 102 | 806 | ..... | 806 | 749 | ..... | 749 |
| Information Technology Systems | 244 | ..... | 244 | 2,296 | ..... | 2,296 | 2,171 | ..... | 2,171 |
| General Operating Expenses | 183 | (**) | 183 | 1,505 | 1 | 1,504 | 1,398 | ..... | 1,398 |
| Other | 115 | ..... | 115 | 666 | ..... | 666 | 683 | ..... | 683 |
| Proprietary Receipts from the Public: | | | | | | | | | |
| National Service Life | ..... | 3 | -3 | ..... | 21 | -21 | ..... | 38 | -38 |
| Other | ..... | 306 | -306 | ..... | 2,186 | -2,186 | ..... | 2,146 | -2,146 |
| Intrabudgetary Transactions | 41 | ..... | 41 | -11 | ..... | -11 | -26 | ..... | -26 |
| **Total--Department of Veterans Affairs** | 18,016 | 420 | 17,596 | 107,865 | 3,184 | 104,682 | 98,460 | 3,262 | 95,198 |
| **Corps of Engineers:** | | | | | | | | | |
| Construction | 168 | ..... | 168 | 1,282 | ..... | 1,282 | 1,482 | ..... | 1,482 |
| Operation and Maintenance | 157 | ..... | 157 | 1,075 | ..... | 1,075 | 1,864 | ..... | 1,864 |
| Flood Control and Coastal Emergencies | 48 | ..... | 48 | 564 | ..... | 564 | 447 | ..... | 447 |
| Harbor Maintenance Trust Fund | 82 | ..... | 82 | 653 | ..... | 653 | ..... | ..... | ..... |
| Rivers and Harbors Contributed Funds | 26 | ..... | 26 | 250 | ..... | 250 | 269 | ..... | 269 |
| Other | 170 | ..... | 170 | 854 | ..... | 854 | 976 | ..... | 976 |
| Proprietary Receipts from the Public | ..... | 28 | -28 | ..... | 290 | -290 | ..... | 593 | -593 |
| Intrabudgetary Transactions | (**) | ..... | (**) | (**) | ..... | (**) | 1 | ..... | 1 |
| **Total--Corps of Engineers** | 650 | 28 | 622 | 4,677 | 290 | 4,387 | 5,039 | 593 | 4,446 |
| **Other Defense Civil Programs:** | | | | | | | | | |
| Military Retirement: | | | | | | | | | |
| Payment to Military Retirement Fund | ..... | ..... | ..... | 72,885 | ..... | 72,885 | 67,733 | ..... | 67,733 |
| Military Retirement Fund | 8,866 | ..... | 8,866 | 41,037 | ..... | 41,037 | 40,248 | ..... | 40,248 |
| Retiree Health Care: | | | | | | | | | |
| Payment to Department of Defense | | | | | | | | | |
| Medicare-Eligible Retiree Health Care Fund | ..... | ..... | ..... | 4,250 | ..... | 4,250 | 6,142 | ..... | 6,142 |
| Department of Defense Medicare-Eligible | | | | | | | | | |
| Retiree Health Care Fund | 700 | ..... | 700 | 6,343 | ..... | 6,343 | 5,565 | ..... | 5,565 |
| Educational Benefits | 35 | ..... | 35 | 282 | ..... | 282 | 289 | ..... | 289 |
| Other | 18 | ..... | 18 | 140 | ..... | 140 | 191 | ..... | 191 |
| Proprietary Receipts from the Public | ..... | 2 | -2 | ..... | 9 | -9 | ..... | 13 | -13 |
| Intrabudgetary Transactions | -1,220 | ..... | -1,220 | -82,227 | ..... | -82,227 | -78,364 | ..... | -78,364 |
| **Total--Other Defense Civil Programs** | 8,399 | 2 | 8,398 | 42,710 | 9 | 42,701 | 41,804 | 13 | 41,791 |
| **Environmental Protection Agency:** | | | | | | | | | |
| Science and Technology | 107 | ..... | 107 | 518 | ..... | 518 | 535 | ..... | 535 |
| Environmental Programs and Management | 103 | ..... | 103 | 1,749 | ..... | 1,749 | 1,735 | ..... | 1,735 |
| State and Tribal Assistance Grants | 263 | ..... | 263 | 2,823 | ..... | 2,823 | 3,347 | ..... | 3,347 |
| Payment to the Hazardous Substance Superfund | ..... | ..... | ..... | 938 | ..... | 938 | 690 | ..... | 690 |
| Hazardous Substance Superfund | 133 | ..... | 133 | 494 | ..... | 494 | 875 | ..... | 875 |
| Other | 36 | (**) | 36 | 100 | 29 | 72 | 178 | 27 | 151 |
| Proprietary Receipts from the Public | ..... | 4 | -4 | ..... | 78 | -78 | ..... | 29 | -29 |
| Intrabudgetary Transactions | -12 | ..... | -12 | -918 | ..... | -918 | -670 | ..... | -670 |
| Offsetting Governmental Receipts | ..... | 3 | -3 | ..... | 17 | -17 | ..... | 27 | -27 |
| **Total--Environmental Protection Agency** | 631 | 7 | 624 | 5,706 | 124 | 5,581 | 6,691 | 83 | 6,607 |
| **Executive Office of the President:** | | | | | | | | | |
| The White House | 4 | ..... | 4 | 36 | ..... | 36 | 36 | ..... | 36 |
| Office of Management and Budget | 6 | ..... | 6 | 55 | ..... | 55 | 58 | ..... | 58 |
| Unanticipated Needs | 1 | ..... | 1 | 9 | ..... | 9 | 7 | ..... | 7 |
| Other | 19 | ..... | 19 | 145 | ..... | 145 | 152 | ..... | 152 |
| Proprietary Receipts from the Public | ..... | (**) | (**) | ..... | (**) | (**) | ..... | (**) | (**) |
| Intrabudgetary Transactions | (**) | ..... | (**) | (**) | ..... | (**) | (**) | ..... | (**) |
| **Total--Executive Office of the President** | 30 | (**) | 30 | 245 | (**) | 244 | 252 | (**) | 252 |

## Table 5. Outlays of the U.S. Government, May 2014 and Other Periods —Continued

[$ millions]

| Classification | This Month Gross Outlays | This Month Applicable Receipts | This Month Outlays | Current Fiscal Year to Date Gross Outlays | Current Fiscal Year to Date Applicable Receipts | Current Fiscal Year to Date Outlays | Prior Fiscal Year to Date Gross Outlays | Prior Fiscal Year to Date Applicable Receipts | Prior Fiscal Year to Date Outlays |
|---|---|---|---|---|---|---|---|---|---|
| **General Services Administration:** | | | | | | | | | |
| Real Property Activities | -118 | ...... | -118 | -417 | ...... | -417 | -131 | ...... | -131 |
| Supply and Technology Activities | 278 | ...... | 278 | 372 | ...... | 372 | -74 | ...... | -74 |
| General Activities | -12 | ...... | -12 | 52 | ...... | 52 | 169 | ...... | 169 |
| Proprietary Receipts from the Public | ...... | 66 | -66 | ...... | 108 | -108 | ...... | 76 | -76 |
| Intrabudgetary Transactions | -2 | ...... | -2 | -6 | ...... | -6 | -5 | ...... | -5 |
| Total--General Services Administration | 146 | 66 | 80 | 1 | 108 | -107 | -42 | 76 | -118 |
| **International Assistance Programs:** | | | | | | | | | |
| Millennium Challenge Corporation | 62 | ...... | 62 | 726 | ...... | 726 | 860 | ...... | 860 |
| International Security Assistance: | | | | | | | | | |
| Pakistan Counterinsurgency Capability Fund | ...... | ...... | ...... | 425 | ...... | 425 | ...... | ...... | ...... |
| Foreign Military Financing Program | 82 | ...... | 82 | 4,433 | ...... | 4,433 | 4,142 | ...... | 4,142 |
| Economic Support Fund | 383 | ...... | 383 | 2,754 | ...... | 2,754 | 2,473 | ...... | 2,473 |
| Other | 154 | 1 | 154 | 745 | 68 | 677 | 651 | 83 | 567 |
| Total--International Security Assistance | 619 | 1 | 619 | 8,357 | 68 | 8,289 | 7,266 | 83 | 7,182 |
| Multilateral Assistance: | | | | | | | | | |
| Contribution to the International Development Association | ...... | ...... | ...... | 5 | ...... | 5 | ...... | ...... | ...... |
| Other | 322 | ...... | 322 | 922 | ...... | 922 | 787 | ...... | 787 |
| Total--Multilateral Assistance | 322 | ...... | 322 | 927 | ...... | 927 | 787 | ...... | 787 |
| Agency for International Development: | | | | | | | | | |
| Development Assistance Program | 191 | ...... | 191 | 1,418 | ...... | 1,418 | 1,345 | ...... | 1,345 |
| Assistance for Europe, Eurasia and Central Asia | 28 | ...... | 28 | 277 | ...... | 277 | 363 | ...... | 363 |
| International Disaster Assistance | 114 | ...... | 114 | 1,062 | ...... | 1,062 | 823 | ...... | 823 |
| Operating Expenses | 180 | ...... | 180 | 811 | ...... | 811 | 910 | ...... | 910 |
| Other | 260 | ...... | 260 | 35 | ...... | 35 | 627 | 246 | 381 |
| Proprietary Receipts from the Public | ...... | (**) | (**) | ...... | 1 | -1 | ...... | 168 | -168 |
| Intrabudgetary Transactions | -41 | ...... | -41 | -37 | ...... | -37 | 15 | ...... | 15 |
| Total--Agency for International Development | 732 | (**) | 731 | 3,565 | 1 | 3,564 | 4,082 | 414 | 3,668 |
| Overseas Private Investment Corporation: | | | | | | | | | |
| Overseas Private Investment Corporation Accounts | 6 | 19 | -13 | 52 | 126 | -74 | 53 | 141 | -88 |
| Proprietary Receipts from the Public | ...... | 23 | -23 | ...... | 98 | -98 | ...... | 142 | -142 |
| Total--Overseas Private Investment Corporation | 6 | 42 | -37 | 52 | 224 | -172 | 53 | 283 | -230 |
| Peace Corps | 26 | (**) | 26 | 236 | (**) | 235 | 225 | (**) | 225 |
| International Monetary Programs | 102 | 1 | 101 | -77 | 1 | -78 | 631 | ...... | 631 |
| Military Sales Programs: | | | | | | | | | |
| Foreign Military Sales Trust Fund | 2,110 | ...... | 2,110 | 17,498 | ...... | 17,498 | 16,568 | ...... | 16,568 |
| Other | 2 | ...... | 2 | 32 | 42 | -10 | 1 | 39 | -38 |
| Proprietary Receipts from the Public | ...... | 2,257 | -2,257 | ...... | 18,526 | -18,526 | ...... | 17,114 | -17,114 |
| Other | 7 | (**) | 7 | 64 | 1 | 63 | 71 | 1 | 70 |
| Total--International Assistance Programs | 3,988 | 2,301 | 1,687 | 31,380 | 18,864 | 12,516 | 30,544 | 17,935 | 12,609 |
| **National Aeronautics and Space Administration:** | | | | | | | | | |
| Science | 392 | ...... | 392 | 3,184 | ...... | 3,184 | 3,016 | ...... | 3,016 |
| Aeronautics | 48 | ...... | 48 | 360 | ...... | 360 | 369 | ...... | 369 |
| Exploration | 317 | ...... | 317 | 2,492 | ...... | 2,492 | 2,772 | ...... | 2,772 |
| Cross Agency Support | 221 | ...... | 221 | 1,806 | ...... | 1,806 | 1,832 | ...... | 1,832 |
| Space Operations | 277 | ...... | 277 | 2,467 | ...... | 2,467 | 2,376 | ...... | 2,376 |
| Other | 88 | ...... | 88 | 764 | ...... | 764 | 688 | ...... | 688 |
| Proprietary Receipts from the Public | ...... | (**) | (**) | ...... | 3 | -3 | ...... | 7 | -7 |
| Intrabudgetary Transactions | (**) | ...... | (**) | -1 | ...... | -1 | -3 | ...... | -3 |
| Total--National Aeronautics and Space Administration | 1,344 | (**) | 1,344 | 11,072 | 3 | 11,069 | 11,051 | 7 | 11,044 |
| **National Science Foundation:** | | | | | | | | | |
| Research and Related Activities | 395 | ...... | 395 | 3,269 | ...... | 3,269 | 3,578 | ...... | 3,578 |
| Education and Human Resources | 78 | ...... | 78 | 556 | ...... | 556 | 531 | ...... | 531 |
| Other | 48 | ...... | 48 | 379 | ...... | 379 | 405 | ...... | 405 |
| Proprietary Receipts from the Public | ...... | 1 | -1 | ...... | 19 | -19 | ...... | 31 | -31 |
| Total--National Science Foundation | 521 | 1 | 520 | 4,204 | 19 | 4,184 | 4,514 | 31 | 4,483 |
| **Office of Personnel Management:** | | | | | | | | | |
| Government Payment for Annuitants, Employees Health and Life Insurance Benefits | 963 | ...... | 963 | 7,493 | ...... | 7,493 | 7,256 | ...... | 7,256 |
| Civil Service Retirement and Disability Fund | 6,609 | ...... | 6,609 | 52,916 | ...... | 52,916 | 51,366 | ...... | 51,366 |
| Employees Life Insurance Fund | 269 | 497 | -228 | 1,964 | 2,829 | -865 | 1,906 | 2,606 | -700 |
| Employees and Retired Employees Health Benefits Fund | 3,847 | 4,253 | -406 | 30,146 | 30,340 | -193 | 28,981 | 30,429 | -1,447 |
| Other | -5 | ...... | -5 | 285 | ...... | 285 | 285 | ...... | 285 |
| Proprietary Receipts from the Public | ...... | (**) | (**) | ...... | 7 | -7 | ...... | 14 | -14 |
| Intrabudgetary Transactions: | | | | | | | | | |
| Postal Service Contributions | ...... | ...... | ...... | -773 | ...... | -773 | -793 | ...... | -793 |
| Civil Service Retirement and Disability Fund: Other | -4 | ...... | -4 | -31 | ...... | -31 | -34 | ...... | -34 |
| Total--Office of Personnel Management | 11,679 | 4,751 | 6,929 | 92,001 | 33,175 | 58,826 | 88,968 | 33,048 | 55,920 |

# Table 5.  Outlays of the U.S. Government, May 2014 and Other Periods —Continued

[$ millions]

| Classification | This Month Gross Outlays | This Month Applicable Receipts | This Month Outlays | Current Fiscal Year to Date Gross Outlays | Current Fiscal Year to Date Applicable Receipts | Current Fiscal Year to Date Outlays | Prior Fiscal Year to Date Gross Outlays | Prior Fiscal Year to Date Applicable Receipts | Prior Fiscal Year to Date Outlays |
|---|---|---|---|---|---|---|---|---|---|
| **Small Business Administration:** | | | | | | | | | |
| Salaries and Expenses | 66 | (**) | 66 | 138 | (**) | 138 | 65 | (**) | 65 |
| Business Loans Program | 8 | (**) | 8 | 577 | 7 | 570 | 1,158 | 1 | 1,157 |
| Disaster Loans Program | 3 | (**) | 2 | 264 | 1 | 263 | 522 | 1 | 521 |
| Other | 11 | 2 | 9 | 44 | 13 | 32 | 22 | 10 | 12 |
| Proprietary Receipts from the Public | ..... | (**) | (**) | ..... | 1,124 | -1,124 | ..... | 1,697 | -1,697 |
| Intrabudgetary Transactions | (**) | ..... | (**) | (**) | ..... | (**) | (**) | ..... | (**) |
| Total--Small Business Administration | 88 | 2 | 86 | 1,024 | 1,145 | -121 | 1,766 | 1,709 | 57 |
| **Social Security Administration:** | | | | | | | | | |
| Payments to Social Security Trust Funds | 17 | ..... | 17 | 18,179 | ..... | 18,179 | 49,894 | ..... | 49,894 |
| Supplemental Security Income Program | 9,405 | ..... | 9,405 | 42,815 | ..... | 42,815 | 41,792 | ..... | 41,792 |
| Federal Old-Age and Survivors Insurance Trust Fund (Off-Budget): | | | | | | | | | |
| Benefit Payments | 58,752 | ..... | 58,752 | 462,075 | ..... | 462,075 | 438,288 | ..... | 438,288 |
| Administrative Expenses | 260 | ..... | 260 | 2,199 | ..... | 2,199 | 2,344 | ..... | 2,344 |
| Total--FOASI Trust Fund | 59,012 | ..... | 59,012 | 464,274 | ..... | 464,274 | 440,631 | ..... | 440,631 |
| Federal Disability Insurance Trust Fund (Off-Budget): | | | | | | | | | |
| Benefit Payments | 11,903 | ..... | 11,903 | 94,100 | ..... | 94,100 | 92,624 | ..... | 92,624 |
| Administrative Expenses | 219 | ..... | 219 | 1,776 | ..... | 1,776 | 1,794 | ..... | 1,794 |
| Total--FDI Trust Fund | 12,123 | ..... | 12,123 | 95,877 | ..... | 95,877 | 94,418 | ..... | 94,418 |
| Other | 28 | ..... | 28 | 237 | ..... | 237 | 202 | ..... | 202 |
| Proprietary Receipts from the Public: | | | | | | | | | |
| On-Budget | ..... | 263 | -263 | ..... | 1,773 | -1,773 | ..... | 1,781 | -1,781 |
| Off-Budget | ..... | 14 | -14 | ..... | 108 | -108 | ..... | 93 | -93 |
| Intrabudgetary Transactions: | | | | | | | | | |
| Off-Budget[1] | -17 | ..... | -17 | -18,178 | ..... | -18,178 | -49,893 | ..... | -49,893 |
| Total--Social Security Administration | 80,568 | 277 | 80,291 | 603,204 | 1,881 | 601,322 | 577,044 | 1,875 | 575,170 |
| **Other Independent Agencies:** | | | | | | | | | |
| Broadcasting Board of Governors | 61 | (**) | 60 | 457 | -1 | 458 | 471 | -1 | 472 |
| Bureau of Consumer Financial Protection | 31 | ..... | 31 | 275 | (**) | 275 | 222 | (**) | 222 |
| Corporation for National and Community Service | 71 | (**) | 71 | 639 | 1 | 637 | 636 | (**) | 635 |
| Corporation for Public Broadcasting | ..... | ..... | ..... | 445 | ..... | 445 | 422 | ..... | 422 |
| District of Columbia: | | | | | | | | | |
| Courts | 24 | ..... | 24 | 193 | ..... | 193 | 218 | ..... | 218 |
| General and Special Payments | 16 | (**) | 16 | 395 | (**) | 394 | 392 | (**) | 392 |
| Equal Employment Opportunity Commission | 23 | (**) | 23 | 217 | 1 | 216 | 223 | 1 | 221 |
| Export-Import Bank of the United States | 1,362 | 955 | 407 | 969 | 934 | 35 | -740 | 4 | -744 |
| Federal Communications Commission: | | | | | | | | | |
| Universal Service Fund | 715 | ..... | 715 | 6,079 | ..... | 6,079 | 6,200 | ..... | 6,200 |
| Spectrum Auction Program Account | (**) | ..... | (**) | 1 | ..... | 1 | (**) | ..... | (**) |
| Other | 35 | 2 | 33 | 175 | 19 | 156 | 211 | 26 | 185 |
| Federal Deposit Insurance Corporation: | | | | | | | | | |
| Deposit Insurance Fund | -435 | ..... | -435 | -6,692 | ..... | -6,692 | -1,148 | -1,103 | -45 |
| FSLIC Resolution Fund | (**) | (**) | (**) | 2 | 3 | -1 | 186 | 6 | 180 |
| Total--Federal Deposit Insurance Corporation | -435 | (**) | -435 | -6,689 | 3 | -6,692 | -962 | -1,097 | 135 |
| Federal Drug Control Programs | 23 | ..... | 23 | 152 | ..... | 152 | 165 | ..... | 165 |
| Federal Housing Finance Agency | 20 | ..... | 20 | 164 | ..... | 164 | 157 | ..... | 157 |
| Intelligence Community Management Account | 47 | ..... | 47 | 320 | ..... | 320 | 325 | ..... | 325 |
| Legal Services Corporation | 24 | ..... | 24 | 201 | ..... | 201 | 231 | ..... | 231 |
| National Archives and Records Administration | 23 | 2 | 21 | 243 | 15 | 228 | 282 | 23 | 259 |
| National Credit Union Administration | 20 | 119 | -99 | -771 | 1,628 | -2,399 | 5,823 | 2,666 | 3,157 |
| National Endowment for the Arts | 9 | (**) | 9 | 88 | (**) | 88 | 96 | (**) | 96 |
| National Endowment for the Humanities | 11 | ..... | 11 | 86 | (**) | 86 | 92 | 1 | 92 |
| Institute of Museum and Library Services | 22 | ..... | 22 | 155 | (**) | 155 | 163 | 1 | 162 |
| National Labor Relations Board | 18 | (**) | 18 | 169 | (**) | 169 | 178 | (**) | 178 |
| Nuclear Regulatory Commission | 80 | 115 | -34 | 646 | 597 | 49 | 670 | 657 | 13 |
| Postal Service: | | | | | | | | | |
| Off-Budget: | | | | | | | | | |
| Public Enterprise Funds | 5,093 | 5,361 | -269 | 48,426 | 50,977 | -2,551 | 49,644 | 52,232 | -2,588 |
| Other | ..... | ..... | ..... | 256 | ..... | 256 | 255 | ..... | 255 |
| Other | (**) | ..... | (**) | 78 | ..... | 78 | 78 | ..... | 78 |

# Table 5. Outlays of the U.S. Government, May 2014 and Other Periods —Continued

[$ millions]

| Classification | This Month | | | Current Fiscal Year to Date | | | Prior Fiscal Year to Date | | |
|---|---|---|---|---|---|---|---|---|---|
| | Gross Outlays | Applicable Receipts | Outlays | Gross Outlays | Applicable Receipts | Outlays | Gross Outlays | Applicable Receipts | Outlays |
| **Other Independent Agencies:—Continued** | | | | | | | | | |
| Railroad Retirement Board: | | | | | | | | | |
| Federal Windfall Subsidy | 3 | ...... | 3 | 25 | ...... | 25 | 29 | ...... | 29 |
| Federal Payments to the Railroad Retirement Accounts | (**) | ...... | (**) | 469 | ...... | 469 | 518 | ...... | 518 |
| Railroad Unemployment Insurance Trust Fund: | | | | | | | | | |
| Benefit Payments | 9 | ...... | 9 | 63 | ...... | 63 | 60 | ...... | 60 |
| Transfer to Administrative Funds | 1 | ...... | 1 | 7 | ...... | 7 | 9 | ...... | 9 |
| Rail Industry Pension Fund: | | | | | | | | | |
| Benefit Payments | 422 | ...... | 422 | 3,343 | ...... | 3,343 | 3,252 | ...... | 3,252 |
| Advances from FOASDI Fund | ...... | ...... | ...... | -499 | ...... | -499 | -955 | ...... | -955 |
| OASDI Certifications | (**) | ...... | (**) | 495 | ...... | 495 | 955 | ...... | 955 |
| Transfer to Administrative Funds | 2 | ...... | 2 | 34 | ...... | 34 | 43 | ...... | 43 |
| Other | 1 | ...... | 1 | 1 | ...... | 1 | 4 | ...... | 4 |
| National Railroad Retirement Investment Trust: | | | | | | | | | |
| Administrative Expenses | 5 | ...... | 5 | 49 | ...... | 49 | 46 | ...... | 46 |
| Transfers to the Railroad Retirement Trust Funds from the National Railroad Retirement Investment Trust | 97 | ...... | 97 | 862 | ...... | 862 | 1,138 | ...... | 1,138 |
| Railroad Social Security Equivalent Benefit Account: | | | | | | | | | |
| Benefit Payments | 571 | ...... | 571 | 4,531 | ...... | 4,531 | 4,451 | ...... | 4,451 |
| Transfer to Administrative Funds | 1 | ...... | 1 | 15 | ...... | 15 | 19 | ...... | 19 |
| Other | 8 | ...... | 8 | 11 | ...... | 11 | 1 | ...... | 1 |
| Proprietary Receipts from the Public | ...... | 150 | -150 | ...... | 2,896 | -2,896 | ...... | 2,649 | -2,649 |
| Intrabudgetary Transactions: | | | | | | | | | |
| Other | -97 | ...... | -97 | -1,331 | ...... | -1,331 | -1,656 | ...... | -1,656 |
| Total--Railroad Retirement Board | 1,022 | 150 | 872 | 8,076 | 2,896 | 5,181 | 7,914 | 2,649 | 5,265 |
| Securities and Exchange Commission | 99 | (**) | 99 | 472 | 1 | 471 | 422 | 1 | 421 |
| Smithsonian Institution | 102 | (**) | 102 | 660 | (**) | 660 | 667 | (**) | 667 |
| Tennessee Valley Authority | 2,986 | 3,113 | -126 | 33,062 | 34,417 | -1,355 | 41,627 | 41,393 | 234 |
| Other | 148 | 21 | 127 | 1,995 | 370 | 1,625 | 1,649 | 276 | 1,373 |
| Total--Other Independent Agencies | 11,651 | 9,837 | 1,813 | 97,633 | 91,858 | 5,775 | 117,731 | 98,832 | 18,899 |
| **Undistributed Offsetting Receipts:** | | | | | | | | | |
| Other Interest | ...... | (**) | (**) | ...... | (**) | (**) | ...... | (**) | (**) |
| Employer Share, Employee Retirement: | | | | | | | | | |
| Department of Health and Human Services: | | | | | | | | | |
| Federal Hospital Insurance Trust Fund: | | | | | | | | | |
| Federal Employer Contributions | -281 | ...... | -281 | -2,295 | ...... | -2,295 | -2,373 | ...... | -2,373 |
| Postal Service Employer Contributions | -49 | ...... | -49 | -397 | ...... | -397 | -392 | ...... | -392 |
| Department of State: | | | | | | | | | |
| Foreign Service Retirement and Disability Fund | -36 | ...... | -36 | -226 | ...... | -226 | -222 | ...... | -222 |
| Other Defense Civil Programs: | | | | | | | | | |
| Military Retirement Fund | -1,769 | ...... | -1,769 | -19,976 | ...... | -19,976 | -20,394 | ...... | -20,394 |
| Department of Defense Medicare-Eligible Retiree Health Care Fund | ...... | ...... | ...... | -7,650 | ...... | -7,650 | -8,529 | ...... | -8,529 |
| Office of Personnel Management: | | | | | | | | | |
| Postal Service Contributions for Benefits | | | | | | | | | |
| Civil Service Retirement and Disability Fund | -2,288 | ...... | -2,288 | -16,247 | ...... | -16,247 | -16,555 | ...... | -16,555 |
| Social Security Administration (Off-Budget): | | | | | | | | | |
| Federal Old-Age and Survivors Insurance Trust Fund: | | | | | | | | | |
| Federal Employer Contributions | -1,140 | ...... | -1,140 | -8,815 | ...... | -8,815 | -9,051 | ...... | -9,051 |
| Federal Disability Insurance Trust Fund: | | | | | | | | | |
| Federal Employer Contributions | -194 | ...... | -194 | -1,498 | ...... | -1,498 | -1,538 | ...... | -1,538 |
| Other | (**) | ...... | (**) | -4 | ...... | -4 | -2 | ...... | -2 |
| Total--Employer Share, Employee Retirement | -5,758 | ...... | -5,758 | -57,108 | ...... | -57,108 | -59,057 | ...... | -59,057 |

# Table 5. Outlays of the U.S. Government, May 2014 and Other Periods —Continued

[$ millions]

| Classification | This Month | | | Current Fiscal Year to Date | | | Prior Fiscal Year to Date | | |
|---|---|---|---|---|---|---|---|---|---|
| | Gross Outlays | Applicable Receipts | Outlays | Gross Outlays | Applicable Receipts | Outlays | Gross Outlays | Applicable Receipts | Outlays |
| **Undistributed Offsetting Receipts:—Continued** | | | | | | | | | |
| Interest Received by Trust Funds: | | | | | | | | | |
| Judicial Branch: | | | | | | | | | |
| Judicial Survivors Annuity Fund | -1 | ...... | -1 | -8 | ...... | -8 | -8 | ...... | -8 |
| Department of Health and Human Services: | | | | | | | | | |
| Federal Hospital Insurance Trust Fund | -37 | ...... | -37 | -4,535 | ...... | -4,535 | -5,182 | ...... | -5,182 |
| Federal Supplementary Medical Insurance Trust Fund | -27 | ...... | -27 | -1,250 | ...... | -1,250 | -1,316 | ...... | -1,316 |
| Department of Homeland Security: | | | | | | | | | |
| Oil Spill Liability Trust Fund | -13 | ...... | -13 | -26 | ...... | -26 | 6 | ...... | 6 |
| Other | (**) | ...... | (**) | -4 | ...... | -4 | -7 | ...... | -7 |
| Department of Labor: | | | | | | | | | |
| Unemployment Trust Fund | -59 | ...... | -59 | -426 | ...... | -426 | -267 | ...... | -267 |
| Department of State: | | | | | | | | | |
| Foreign Service Retirement and Disability Fund | -1 | ...... | -1 | -327 | ...... | -327 | -341 | ...... | -341 |
| Department of Transportation: | | | | | | | | | |
| Airport and Airway Trust Fund | -9 | ...... | -9 | -138 | ...... | -138 | -112 | ...... | -112 |
| Department of Veterans Affairs: | | | | | | | | | |
| National Service Life Insurance Fund | -2 | ...... | -2 | -144 | ...... | -144 | -166 | ...... | -166 |
| United States Government Life Insurance Fund | (**) | ...... | (**) | (**) | ...... | (**) | (**) | ...... | (**) |
| Corps of Engineers | -18 | ...... | -18 | -80 | ...... | -80 | -135 | ...... | -135 |
| Other Defense Civil Programs: | | | | | | | | | |
| Military Retirement Fund | -2,957 | ...... | -2,957 | -5,904 | ...... | -5,904 | 224 | ...... | 224 |
| Educational Benefits Fund | -17 | ...... | -17 | -55 | ...... | -55 | -55 | ...... | -55 |
| Armed Forces Retirement Home | -1 | ...... | -1 | -2 | ...... | -2 | -2 | ...... | -2 |
| Environmental Protection Agency | (**) | ...... | (**) | -35 | ...... | -35 | -37 | ...... | -37 |
| Office of Personnel Management: | | | | | | | | | |
| Civil Service Retirement and Disability Fund | -51 | ...... | -51 | -15,756 | ...... | -15,756 | -16,278 | ...... | -16,278 |
| Social Security Administration (Off-Budget): | | | | | | | | | |
| Federal Old-Age and Survivors Insurance Trust Fund | -81 | ...... | -81 | -48,185 | ...... | -48,185 | -50,091 | ...... | -50,091 |
| Federal Disability Insurance Trust Fund | -28 | ...... | -28 | -2,178 | ...... | -2,178 | -3,044 | ...... | -3,044 |
| Independent Agencies: | | | | | | | | | |
| Railroad Retirement Board | -3 | ...... | -3 | -23 | ...... | -23 | -37 | ...... | -37 |
| Other | -2 | ...... | -2 | -13 | ...... | -13 | -8 | ...... | -8 |
| Other | -32 | ...... | -32 | -103 | ...... | -103 | -103 | ...... | -103 |
| Total—Interest Received by Trust Funds | -3,340 | ...... | -3,340 | -79,194 | ...... | -79,194 | -76,962 | ...... | -76,962 |
| Rents and Royalties on the Outer Continental Shelf Lands | ...... | 213 | -213 | ...... | 3,986 | -3,986 | ...... | 5,790 | -5,790 |
| Sale of Major Assets | ...... | ...... | ...... | ...... | ...... | ...... | ...... | 2,588 | -2,588 |
| Total—Undistributed Offsetting Receipts | -9,098 | 213 | -9,311 | -136,302 | 3,986 | -140,288 | -136,019 | 8,379 | -144,398 |
| **Total Outlays** | 365,961 | 36,101 | 329,860 | 2,707,551 | 336,251 | 2,371,301 | 2,734,569 | 307,729 | 2,426,840 |
| Total On-Budget | 291,194 | 30,726 | 260,468 | 2,177,572 | 285,165 | 1,892,407 | 2,263,238 | 255,403 | 2,007,834 |
| Total Off-Budget | 74,767 | 5,375 | 69,392 | 529,979 | 51,086 | 478,894 | 471,332 | 52,326 | 419,006 |
| **Total Surplus (+) or Deficit** | | | -129,971 | | | -436,382 | | | -626,325 |
| Total On-Budget | | | -119,679 | | | -451,204 | | | -646,558 |
| Total Off-Budget | | | -10,292 | | | +14,822 | | | +20,233 |

## MEMORANDUM
### Receipts Offset Against Outlays (In Millions)

| | Current Fiscal Year to Date | Comparable Period Prior Fiscal Year |
|---|---|---|
| Proprietary Receipts | 188,106 | 145,932 |
| Intrabudgetary Transactions | 441,048 | 472,536 |
| Governmental Receipts | 6,139 | 5,974 |
| Total Receipts Offset Against Outlays | 635,292 | 624,441 |

[1]Includes FICA and SECA tax credits, non-contributory military service credits, special benefits for the aged, and credit for the unnegotiated OASI benefit checks.

... No Transactions
(**) Less than $500,000
Note: Details may not add to totals due to rounding.

# Table 6. Means of Financing the Deficit or Disposition of Surplus by the U.S. Government, May 2014 and Other Periods
[$ millions]

| Assets and Liabilities Directly Related to Budget Off-Budget Activity | Net Transactions (-) denotes net reduction of either liability or asset accounts | | | Account Balances Current Fiscal Year | | |
|---|---|---|---|---|---|---|
| | This Month | Fiscal Year to Date | | Beginning of | | Close of This Month |
| | | This Year | Prior Year | This Year | This Month | |
| **Liability Accounts:** | | | | | | |
| Borrowing from the Public: | | | | | | |
| Treasury Securities, Issued Under General Financing Authorities: | | | | | | |
| Debt Held by the Public | 34,562 | 561,751 | 627,565 | 11,976,279 | 12,503,468 | 12,538,030 |
| Intragovernmental Holdings | -26,041 | 217,024 | 45,016 | 4,761,904 | 5,004,969 | 4,978,928 |
| Total Treasury Securities Outstanding | 8,521 | 778,775 | 672,581 | 16,738,184 | 17,508,437 | 17,516,958 |
| Plus Premium on Treasury Securities | -17 | -1,526 | 4,826 | 36,420 | 34,911 | 34,894 |
| Less Discount on Treasury Securities | -273 | 6,650 | 316 | 82,916 | 89,839 | 89,566 |
| Total Treasury Securities Net of Premium and Discount | 8,777 | 770,599 | 677,090 | 16,691,687 | 17,453,509 | 17,462,286 |
| Agency Securities, Issued Under Special Financing Authorities (See Schedule B; for Other Agency Borrowing, See Schedule C) | -98 | -1,227 | 375 | 25,103 | 23,974 | 23,876 |
| Total Federal Securities | 8,679 | 769,372 | 677,464 | 16,716,791 | 17,477,484 | 17,486,162 |
| Deduct: | | | | | | |
| Federal Securities Held as Investments of Government Accounts (See Schedule D) | -26,103 | 221,855 | 44,521 | 4,757,211 | 5,005,168 | 4,979,066 |
| Less Discount on Federal Securities Held as Investments of Government Accounts | -90 | 4,691 | -1,047 | 22,292 | 27,074 | 26,984 |
| Net Federal Securities Held as Investments of Government Accounts | -26,013 | 217,163 | 45,569 | 4,734,919 | 4,978,095 | 4,952,082 |
| Total Borrowing from the Public | 34,692 | 552,208 | 631,896 | 11,981,872 | 12,499,389 | 12,534,080 |
| Accrued Interest Payable to the Public | -12,441 | -291 | -14,020 | 51,231 | 63,382 | 50,940 |
| Allocations of Special Drawing Rights | -326 | 226 | -1,533 | 54,177 | 54,728 | 54,403 |
| Deposit Funds | -3,433 | -116,334 | 30,800 | 131,385 | 18,484 | 15,051 |
| Miscellaneous Liability Accounts (Includes Checks Outstanding Etc.) | -2,902 | 1,904 | 54 | 8,934 | 13,741 | 10,838 |
| **Total Liability Accounts** | 15,589 | 437,713 | 647,196 | 12,227,600 | 12,649,723 | 12,665,313 |
| **Asset Accounts (Deduct)** | | | | | | |
| Cash and Monetary Assets: | | | | | | |
| U.S. Treasury Operating Cash:[1] | | | | | | |
| Federal Reserve Account | -119,449 | -59,492 | -50,765 | 88,386 | 148,343 | 28,894 |
| Balance | -119,449 | -59,492 | -50,765 | 88,386 | 148,343 | 28,894 |
| Special Drawing Rights: | | | | | | |
| Total Holdings | -322 | 251 | -1,537 | 54,966 | 55,539 | 55,217 |
| SDR Certificates Issued to Federal Reserve Banks | ...... | ...... | ...... | -5,200 | -5,200 | -5,200 |
| Balance | -322 | 251 | -1,537 | 49,766 | 50,339 | 50,017 |
| Reserve Position on the U.S. Quota in the IMF: | | | | | | |
| U.S. Subscription to International Monetary Fund: | | | | | | |
| Direct Quota Payments | ...... | ...... | ...... | 54,424 | 54,424 | 54,424 |
| Maintenance of Value Adjustments | -388 | 269 | -1,829 | 10,298 | 10,956 | 10,567 |
| Letter of Credit Issued to IMF | 742 | -3,640 | -2,895 | -43,827 | -48,209 | -47,467 |
| Dollar Deposits with the IMF | -14 | (**) | -1 | -152 | -138 | -152 |
| Receivable/payable (-) for Interim Maintenance of Value Adjustments | 292 | -187 | 1,204 | -874 | -1,352 | -1,060 |
| Balance | 632 | -3,558 | -3,521 | 19,870 | 15,680 | 16,312 |
| Loans to International Monetary Fund | 476 | 391 | 1,394 | 13,763 | 13,678 | 14,154 |
| Other Cash and Monetary Assets | -543 | -434 | -436 | 26,110 | 26,219 | 25,676 |
| Total Cash and Monetary Assets | -119,206 | -62,842 | -54,864 | 197,895 | 254,258 | 135,052 |
| Non-Federal Securities of the National Railroad Retirement Investment Trust | 41 | 1,831 | 1,585 | 23,347 | 25,136 | 25,178 |
| Net Activity, Guaranteed Loan Financing (See Schedule E) | 3,247 | 7,941 | 13,450 | -10,369 | -5,674 | -2,427 |
| Net Activity, Direct Loan Financing (See Schedule E) | 2,006 | 53,156 | 59,913 | 946,711 | 997,861 | 999,867 |
| Miscellaneous Asset Accounts | -470 | 237 | 788 | -409 | 298 | -172 |
| **Total Asset Accounts** | -114,382 | 323 | 20,872 | 1,157,175 | 1,271,879 | 1,157,498 |
| **Excess of Liabilities (+) or Assets (-)** | 129,971 | 437,390 | 626,325 | 11,070,425 | 11,377,844 | 11,507,815 |
| Transactions Not Applied to Current Year's Surplus or Deficit (See Schedule A for Details) | ...... | -1,008 | ...... | ...... | -1,008 | -1,008 |
| **Total Budget and Off-Budget Federal Entities (Financing of Deficit (+) or Disposition of Surplus (-))** | 129,971 | 436,382 | 626,325 | 11,070,425 | 11,376,836 | 11,506,807 |

Major sources of information used to determine Treasury's operating cash balance include Federal Reserve Banks, Treasury Regional Finance Centers, Internal Revenue Service Centers, various electronic systems, and information on the Public Debt. Information is presented on a modified cash basis. Deposits are reflected as received and withdrawals are reflected as processed.

... No Transactions
(**) Less than $500,000
Note: Details may not add to totals due to rounding.

**Table 6. Schedule A-Analysis of Change in Excess of Liabilities of the U.S. Government, May 2014 and Other Periods**

[$ millions]

| Classification | This Month | Fiscal Year to Date | |
|---|---|---|---|
| | | This Year | Prior Year |
| **Excess of Liabilities Beginning of Period:** | | | |
| Based on Composition of Unified Budget in Preceding Period | 11,377,844 | 11,070,433 | 10,390,656 |
| Adjustments During Current Fiscal Year for Changes in Composition of Unified Budget: | | | |
| Revisions by Federal Agencies to the Prior Budget Results | ..... | -8 | -151 |
| Excess of Liabilities Beginning of Period (Current Basis) | 11,377,844 | 11,070,425 | 10,390,505 |
| **Budget Surplus (-) or Deficit:** | | | |
| Based on Composition of Unified Budget in Prior Fiscal Year | 129,971 | 436,382 | 626,325 |
| Total Surplus (-) or Deficit (Table 2) | 129,971 | 436,382 | 626,325 |
| Total-On-Budget (Table 2) | 119,679 | 451,204 | 646,558 |
| Total-Off-Budget (Table 2) | 10,292 | -14,822 | -20,233 |
| **Transactions Not Applied to Current Year's Surplus or Deficit:** | | | |
| Reclassification of Aged Unreconciled Accounts | ..... | 1,008 | ..... |
| Total-Transactions Not Applied to Current Year's Surplus or Deficit | ..... | 1,008 | ..... |
| **Excess of Liabilities Close of Period** | 11,507,815 | 11,507,815 | 11,016,830 |

... No Transactions

Note: Details may not add to totals due to rounding.

---

**Table 6. Schedule B-Securities Issued by Federal Agencies Under Special Financing Authorities, May 2014 and Other Periods**

[$ millions]

| Classification | Net Transactions (-) denotes net reduction of liability accounts | | | Account Balances Current Fiscal Year | | |
|---|---|---|---|---|---|---|
| | This Month | Fiscal Year to Date | | Beginning of | | Close of This Month |
| | | This Year | Prior Year | This Year | This Month | |
| **Agency Securities, Issued Under Special Financing Authorities:** | | | | | | |
| Obligations Guaranteed by the United States, Issued By: | | | | | | |
| Department of Housing and Urban Development: | | | | | | |
| Federal Housing Administration | ..... | ..... | ..... | 19 | 19 | 19 |
| Obligations Not Guaranteed by the United States, Issued By: | | | | | | |
| Legislative Branch: | | | | | | |
| Architect of the Capitol | 1 | -10 | -1 | 130 | 119 | 119 |
| Independent Agencies: | | | | | | |
| Federal Communications Commission | ..... | ..... | ..... | (**) | (**) | (**) |
| National Archives and Records Administration | ..... | -9 | -8 | 134 | 125 | 125 |
| Tennessee Valley Authority | -99 | -1,208 | 384 | 24,821 | 23,712 | 23,613 |
| Total Agency Securities | -98 | -1,227 | 375 | 25,103 | 23,974 | 23,876 |

... No Transactions

(**) Less than $500,000.

Note: Details may not add to totals due to rounding.

## Table 6. Schedule C (Memorandum)-Federal Agency Borrowing Financed Through the Issue of Treasury Securities, May 2014 and Other Periods

[$ millions]

| Classification | Transactions | | | Account Balances Current Fiscal Year | | |
|---|---|---|---|---|---|---|
| | This Month | Fiscal Year to Date | | Beginning of | | Close of This Month |
| | | This Year | Prior Year | This Year | This Month | |
| **Borrowing from the Treasury:** | | | | | | |
| Department of Agriculture: | | | | | | |
| Farm Service Agency: | | | | | | |
| Commodity Credit Corporation | 554 | 1,590 | 1,706 | 3,729 | 4,765 | 5,319 |
| Agricultural Credit Insurance Fund | ...... | 733 | 102 | 7,433 | 8,166 | 8,166 |
| Farm Storage Facility Loans | 2 | 218 | 262 | 970 | 1,186 | 1,187 |
| Emergency Boll Weevil Loan Fund | ...... | ...... | ...... | 3 | 3 | 3 |
| Rural Housing Service: | | | | | | |
| Rural Housing Insurance | 75 | 380 | 355 | 16,566 | 16,872 | 16,946 |
| Rural Community Facility Loans Fund | 70 | -72 | 410 | 5,291 | 5,149 | 5,219 |
| Multifamily Housing Revitalization Loan Account | 1 | -47 | 31 | 255 | 207 | 208 |
| Rural Business - Cooperative Service: | | | | | | |
| Rural Business and Industry Loans | (**) | -18 | -10 | 67 | 49 | 49 |
| Rural Development Loan Fund | 1 | -13 | 5 | 320 | 307 | 308 |
| Rural Economic Development Loan Fund | 4 | 2 | 16 | 140 | 139 | 143 |
| Renewable Energy Guaranteed Loan Account | ...... | ...... | -1 | (**) | (**) | (**) |
| Rural Microenterprise Investment Loans | (**) | 3 | 3 | 18 | 21 | 21 |
| Biorefinery Assistance Loan Account | ...... | ...... | ...... | 8 | 8 | 8 |
| Rural Utilities Service: | | | | | | |
| Rural Water and Waste Disposal Fund | 73 | -568 | 437 | 12,193 | 11,552 | 11,625 |
| Rural Electrification and Telecommunications Fund | 60 | -690 | -209 | 12,232 | 11,483 | 11,543 |
| Rural Telephone Bank | ...... | -62 | -14 | 354 | 292 | 292 |
| Distance Learning and Telemedicine Program | 9 | -51 | 189 | 1,290 | 1,230 | 1,239 |
| Foreign Agricultural Service | ...... | ...... | ...... | 908 | 908 | 908 |
| Department of Commerce: | | | | | | |
| Departmental Management: | | | | | | |
| Emergency Steel Guaranteed Loan Fund | ...... | ...... | 10 | 39 | 39 | 39 |
| National Oceanic and Atmospheric Administration: | | | | | | |
| Fisheries Finance | 1 | 30 | 22 | 525 | 554 | 555 |
| State and Local Implementation Fund | ...... | ...... | 2 | 12 | 12 | 12 |
| Department of Defense - Military Programs: | | | | | | |
| Arms Initiative Loans | ...... | ...... | ...... | (**) | (**) | (**) |
| Family Housing Improvement Loans | ...... | 83 | 175 | 1,173 | 1,256 | 1,256 |
| Department of Education: | | | | | | |
| College Housing and Academic Facilities Loans | ...... | (**) | (**) | 37 | 37 | 37 |
| Federal Direct Student Loans | ...... | 104,327 | 111,942 | 736,960 | 841,287 | 841,287 |
| Teach Grant Loans | ...... | 54 | 71 | 485 | 539 | 539 |
| Temporary Student Loan Purchase Authority | ...... | -178 | 407 | 70,559 | 70,381 | 70,381 |
| Federal Family Education Loans | ...... | ...... | ...... | 43,254 | 43,254 | 43,254 |
| Department of Energy: | | | | | | |
| Bonneville Power Administration Fund | 44 | 365 | 396 | 3,885 | 4,206 | 4,250 |
| Western Area Power Administration - Recovery Act | ...... | 31 | -135 | 58 | 89 | 89 |
| Title 17 Innovative Technology Loans | ...... | 73 | ...... | ...... | 73 | 73 |
| Advanced Technology Vehicles Manufacturing Loans | ...... | 32 | ...... | 24 | 56 | 56 |
| Department of Health and Human Services: | | | | | | |
| Consumer Operated and Oriented Plan Program Contingency Fund | ...... | 47 | ...... | 4 | 51 | 51 |
| Consumer Operated and Oriented Plan | ...... | 249 | 516 | 535 | 784 | 784 |
| Department of Homeland Security: | | | | | | |
| National Flood Insurance Fund | ...... | ...... | 6,250 | 24,000 | 24,000 | 24,000 |
| Disaster Assistance Loan Fund | (*) | 21 | 1 | 76 | 97 | 97 |
| Department of Housing and Urban Development: | | | | | | |
| Public and Indian Housing Programs: | | | | | | |
| Low-Rent Public Housing - Loans and Other Expenses | ...... | ...... | 30 | 115 | 115 | 115 |
| Native Hawaiian Housing Loans | ...... | ...... | ...... | 6 | 6 | 6 |
| Housing Programs: | | | | | | |
| Emergency Homeowners' Relief Fund | ...... | (**) | -2 | 3 | 3 | 3 |
| Federal Housing Administration | ...... | ...... | ...... | 25,940 | 25,940 | 25,940 |
| Green Retrofit Program for Multifamily Housing-Recovery Act | ...... | ...... | ...... | 15 | 15 | 15 |

# Table 6. Schedule C (Memorandum)-Federal Agency Borrowing Financed Through the Issue of Treasury Securities, May 2014 and Other Periods —Continued

[$ millions]

| Classification | Transactions | | | Account Balances Current Fiscal Year | | |
|---|---|---|---|---|---|---|
| | This Month | Fiscal Year to Date | | Beginning of | | Close of |
| | | This Year | Prior Year | This Year | This Month | This Month |
| Borrowing from the Treasury:—Continued | | | | | | |
| Department of the Interior: | | | | | | |
| Helium Fund | ..... | -44 | ..... | 44 | ..... | ..... |
| Bureau of Reclamation Loan Fund | (**) | (**) | ..... | 35 | 35 | 35 |
| Bureau of Indian Affairs | (**) | (**) | 4 | 9 | 9 | 9 |
| Assistance to American Samoa Loan Fund | ..... | 1 | ..... | 9 | 10 | 10 |
| Department of Labor: | | | | | | |
| Black Lung Disability Trust Fund | ..... | ..... | ..... | 5,036 | 5,036 | 5,036 |
| Department of State: | | | | | | |
| Repatriation Loans | ..... | 1 | (**) | 3 | 4 | 4 |
| Department of Transportation: | | | | | | |
| Federal Aviation Administration: | | | | | | |
| Federal Highway Administration: | | | | | | |
| Transportation Infrastructure Finance and Innovation Fund | 91 | 999 | 568 | 6,105 | 7,013 | 7,103 |
| Federal Railroad Administration: | | | | | | |
| Railroad Rehabilitation and Improvement Loan Fund | 7 | 45 | 71 | 816 | 854 | 861 |
| Other | ..... | ..... | ..... | (**) | (**) | (**) |
| Maritime Administration: | | | | | | |
| Ocean Freight Differential | ..... | ..... | -33 | ..... | ..... | ..... |
| Maritime Guaranteed Loan (Title XI) Fund | ..... | ..... | ..... | 37 | 37 | 37 |
| Department of Treasury: | | | | | | |
| Departmental Offices: | | | | | | |
| Community Development Financial Institutions Fund | 8 | 15 | 5 | 38 | 45 | 52 |
| Temporary Credit and Liquidity Program | ..... | ..... | ..... | 8,865 | 8,865 | 8,865 |
| Troubled Assets Insurance Financing Fund | ..... | ..... | -760 | ..... | ..... | ..... |
| Troubled Asset Relief Program | ..... | -2,704 | -31,709 | 11,949 | 9,244 | 9,244 |
| Small Business Lending Financing Fund | ..... | ..... | ..... | 3,712 | 3,712 | 3,712 |
| Federal Financing Bank Revolving Fund | 797 | -5,369 | 4,079 | 63,061 | 56,896 | 57,692 |
| Department of Veterans Affairs: | | | | | | |
| Veterans Housing Benefit Program Fund | ..... | 242 | 169 | 681 | 923 | 923 |
| Native American Veteran Housing Fund | ..... | 4 | 9 | 68 | 72 | 72 |
| Vocational Rehabilitation Loan Fund | ..... | 1 | 3 | 2 | 4 | 4 |
| Corps of Engineers: | | | | | | |
| Washington Aqueduct | ..... | (**) | (**) | 2 | 2 | 2 |
| Environmental Protection Agency: | | | | | | |
| Abatement, Control, and Compliance Loan Program | ..... | ..... | ..... | (**) | (**) | (**) |
| General Services Administration: | | | | | | |
| International Assistance Program: | | | | | | |
| International Security Assistance: | | | | | | |
| Military Debt Reduction | ..... | ..... | ..... | 36 | 36 | 36 |
| Agency for International Development: | | | | | | |
| International Debt Reduction | ..... | ..... | ..... | 478 | 478 | 478 |
| Development Credit Authority Loan Fund | ..... | ..... | ..... | 3 | 3 | 3 |
| Overseas Private Investment Corporation | 32 | 248 | 375 | 2,293 | 2,509 | 2,541 |
| International Monetary Programs | 1 | 1 | 1,800 | 7,846 | 7,846 | 7,847 |
| Small Business Administration: | | | | | | |
| Business Loan Fund | 438 | 428 | -508 | 1,432 | 1,423 | 1,861 |
| Disaster Loan Fund | ..... | 340 | 1,111 | 6,656 | 6,996 | 6,996 |
| Independent Agencies: | | | | | | |
| Export-Import Bank of the United States | ..... | 2,250 | 4,892 | 18,102 | 20,352 | 20,352 |
| Federal Communications Commission: | | | | | | |
| Spectrum Auction Loan Fund | ..... | (**) | (**) | (**) | ..... | ..... |
| National Credit Union Administration | ..... | -1,825 | 1,525 | 4,725 | 2,900 | 2,900 |
| Presidio Trust Fund | ..... | ..... | ..... | 50 | 50 | 50 |
| Railroad Retirement Board: | | | | | | |
| Social Security Equivalent Benefit Account | 293 | 2,548 | 2,603 | 3,587 | 5,842 | 6,135 |
| Smithsonian Institution: | | | | | | |
| John F. Kennedy Center Parking Facilities | ..... | ..... | ..... | 20 | 20 | 20 |
| Total Agency Borrowing from the Treasury Financed Through Treasury Securities Issued | 2,559 | 103,722 | 107,171 | 1,115,182 | 1,216,345 | 1,218,904 |

## Table 6. Schedule C (Memorandum)-Federal Agency Borrowing Financed Through the Issue of Treasury Securities, May 2014 and Other Periods —Continued

[$ millions]

| Classification | Transactions | | | Account Balances Current Fiscal Year | | |
| --- | --- | --- | --- | --- | --- | --- |
| | This Month | Fiscal Year to Date | | Beginning of | | Close of This Month |
| | | This Year | Prior Year | This Year | This Month | |
| Borrowing from the Federal Financing Bank: | | | | | | |
| Department of Agriculture: | | | | | | |
| Rural Utilities Service: | | | | | | |
| Rural Electrification and Telecommunications Fund | 731 | 1,754 | 1,596 | 40,638 | 41,662 | 42,393 |
| Department of Education: | | | | | | |
| Historically Black College and University Capital | | | | | | |
| Financing Fund | 12 | 69 | 98 | 1,129 | 1,185 | 1,197 |
| Department of Energy: | | | | | | |
| Title 17 Innovative Technology Loans | -29 | 1,308 | 2,348 | 7,894 | 9,231 | 9,202 |
| Advanced Technology Vehicles Manufacturing | ...... | -477 | -666 | 5,962 | 5,485 | 5,485 |
| Department of Health and Human Services: | | | | | | |
| Health Maintenance Organization Loan and | | | | | | |
| Loan Guarantee Fund | ...... | ...... | ...... | (**) | (**) | (**) |
| Department of Transportation: | | | | | | |
| Railroad Rehabilitation and Improvement Loan Fund | ...... | (**) | (**) | 1 | (**) | (**) |
| Department of Veterans Affairs: | | | | | | |
| Guaranteed Transitional Housing for Homeless Veterans | ...... | (**) | (**) | 5 | 5 | 5 |
| General Services Administration: | | | | | | |
| Federal Buildings Fund | (**) | -60 | -56 | 1,733 | 1,673 | 1,673 |
| International Assistance Program: | | | | | | |
| Foreign Military Financing Program | ...... | -47 | -58 | 80 | 33 | 33 |
| Small Business Administration: | | | | | | |
| Business Loan Fund | ...... | ...... | (**) | ...... | ...... | ...... |
| Independent Agencies: | | | | | | |
| Postal Service | ...... | ...... | ...... | 15,000 | 15,000 | 15,000 |
| Total Borrowing from the Federal Financing Bank | 715 | 2,547 | 3,262 | 72,441 | 74,273 | 74,988 |

Note: This table includes lending by the Federal Financing Bank accomplished by the purchase of agency financial assets, by the acquisition of agency debt securities, and by direct loans on behalf of an agency. The Federal Financing Bank borrows from Treasury and issues its own securities and in turn may loan these funds to agencies in lieu of agencies borrowing directly through Treasury or issuing their own securities.

... No Transactions

(**) Less than $500,000

Note: Details may not add to totals due to rounding.

This Page Left Blank Intentionally

## Table 6. Schedule D-Investments of Federal Government Accounts in Federal Securities, May 2014 and Other Periods

[$ millions]

| Classification | Net Purchases or Sales (-) | | | Securities Held as Investments Current Fiscal Year | | |
|---|---|---|---|---|---|---|
| | This Month | Fiscal Year to Date | | Beginning of | | Close of |
| | | This Year | Prior Year | This Year | This Month | This Month |
| **Federal Funds:** | | | | | | |
| Department of Agriculture | -8 | 87 | 62 | 138 | 234 | 225 |
| Department of Commerce | ...... | 2 | 2 | ...... | 2 | 2 |
| Department of Defense-Military Programs: | | | | | | |
| Defense Cooperation Account | ...... | (**) | ...... | 8 | 8 | 8 |
| Department of Energy | 66 | 658 | 687 | 54,770 | 55,362 | 55,427 |
| Department of Health and Human Services | ...... | 3 | 3 | 2,098 | 2,101 | 2,101 |
| Department of Housing and Urban Development: | | | | | | |
| Housing Programs: | | | | | | |
| Federal Housing Administration Fund | 755 | 2,912 | 9,632 | 3 | 2,160 | 2,915 |
| Government National Mortgage Association: | | | | | | |
| Guarantees of Mortgage-Backed Securities | (**) | -336 | -138 | 1,812 | 1,475 | 1,475 |
| Department of the Interior | -177 | -358 | 828 | 7,513 | 7,332 | 7,155 |
| Department of Labor | -72 | -329 | 596 | 17,768 | 17,511 | 17,439 |
| Department of Transportation | 78 | 173 | 134 | 1,980 | 2,074 | 2,152 |
| Department of the Treasury | 19 | -759 | 1,131 | 26,049 | 25,272 | 25,290 |
| Department of Veterans Affairs: | | | | | | |
| Veterans Reopened Insurance Fund | -3 | -19 | -20 | 226 | 210 | 207 |
| Servicemen's Group Life Insurance Fund | ...... | (**) | (**) | 1 | 1 | 1 |
| Other Defense Civil Programs: | | | | | | |
| Uniformed Services Retiree Health Care Fund | 727 | 11,974 | 13,609 | 188,664 | 199,911 | 200,638 |
| Office of Personnel Management: | | | | | | |
| Postal Service Contributions | ...... | 5,375 | 793 | 42,324 | 47,699 | 47,699 |
| Independent Agencies: | | | | | | |
| Federal Deposit Insurance Corporation: | | | | | | |
| Deposit Insurance Fund | 439 | 6,822 | 38 | 36,864 | 43,247 | 43,686 |
| FSLIC Resolution Fund | (**) | 1 | 1 | 825 | 826 | 826 |
| Federal Housing Finance Agency | -17 | 59 | 59 | 72 | 148 | 131 |
| National Credit Union Administration | 97 | 587 | -1,628 | 11,200 | 11,690 | 11,787 |
| Postal Service | 191 | 2,336 | 762 | 2,860 | 5,005 | 5,196 |
| Tennessee Valley Authority | (**) | (**) | (**) | 25 | 25 | 25 |
| Other | 75 | 628 | 357 | 15,806 | 16,359 | 16,434 |
| Other | 281 | 1,550 | 674 | 10,908 | 12,178 | 12,459 |
| Total Treasury Securities | 2,451 | 31,366 | 27,579 | 421,914 | 450,829 | 453,280 |
| **Total Federal Funds** | 2,451 | 31,366 | 27,579 | 421,914 | 450,829 | 453,280 |
| **Trust Funds:** | | | | | | |
| Legislative Branch: | | | | | | |
| Library of Congress | (**) | 4 | -16 | 26 | 30 | 30 |
| United States Tax Court | (**) | (**) | (**) | 11 | 11 | 11 |
| Other | -1 | -1 | 2 | 31 | 32 | 31 |
| Judicial Branch: | | | | | | |
| Judicial Retirement Funds | -2 | 87 | 84 | 1,024 | 1,113 | 1,111 |
| Department of Agriculture | 7 | 61 | 78 | ...... | 54 | 61 |
| Department of Defense-Military Programs: | | | | | | |
| Voluntary Separation Incentive Fund | -4 | 6 | 10 | 269 | 279 | 275 |
| Other | 5 | -32 | 73 | 903 | 867 | 871 |
| Department of Health and Human Services: | | | | | | |
| Federal Hospital Insurance Trust Fund | -10,972 | -6,718 | -23,591 | 206,010 | 210,263 | 199,291 |
| Federal Supplementary Medical Insurance Trust Fund | -8,466 | 745 | -8,861 | 67,385 | 76,596 | 68,131 |
| Other | 7 | 82 | -8 | 3,272 | 3,347 | 3,354 |

# Table 6. Schedule D-Investments of Federal Government Accounts in Federal Securities, May 2014 and Other Periods —Continued

[$ millions]

| Classification | Net Purchases or Sales (-) | | | Securities Held as Investments Current Fiscal Year | | |
| --- | --- | --- | --- | --- | --- | --- |
| | This Month | Fiscal Year to Date | | Beginning of | | Close of This Month |
| | | This Year | Prior Year | This Year | This Month | |
| Trust Funds:—Continued | | | | | | |
| Department of Homeland Security | 14 | 349 | 418 | 5,080 | 5,415 | 5,429 |
| Department of the Interior | (**) | 1 | -25 | 11 | 13 | 12 |
| Department of Labor: | | | | | | |
| Unemployment Trust Fund | 9,504 | 7,538 | 12,592 | 29,478 | 27,511 | 37,016 |
| Other | -6 | -17 | -19 | 65 | 54 | 48 |
| Department of State: | | | | | | |
| Foreign Service Retirement and Disability Fund | 44 | 120 | 146 | 17,364 | 17,440 | 17,484 |
| Other | (**) | (**) | 3 | 44 | 43 | 43 |
| Department of Transportation: | | | | | | |
| Airport and Airway Trust Fund | -5 | 54 | 1,687 | 11,808 | 11,867 | 11,862 |
| Highway Trust Fund | 114 | 8,009 | 2,347 | 1,957 | 9,852 | 9,966 |
| Department of Treasury | -74 | 190 | 104 | 1,685 | 1,949 | 1,876 |
| Department of Veterans Affairs: | | | | | | |
| General Post Fund, National Homes | -9 | (**) | 20 | 86 | 95 | 86 |
| National Service Life Insurance | -74 | -476 | -486 | 6,256 | 5,854 | 5,780 |
| United States Government Life Insurance Fund | (**) | -2 | -2 | 10 | 8 | 8 |
| Veterans Special Life Insurance Fund | -13 | -50 | -40 | 1,914 | 1,877 | 1,864 |
| Corps of Engineers | 64 | 414 | 1,123 | 7,866 | 8,216 | 8,280 |
| Other Defense Civil Programs: | | | | | | |
| Military Retirement Fund | -4,433 | 61,784 | 47,372 | 421,327 | 487,544 | 483,111 |
| Other | -13 | -185 | -182 | 1,844 | 1,672 | 1,659 |
| Environmental Protection Agency | -66 | 636 | -13 | 4,510 | 5,212 | 5,146 |
| National Aeronautics and Space Administration | ...... | (**) | (**) | 15 | 15 | 15 |
| Office of Personnel Management: | | | | | | |
| Civil Service Retirement and Disability Fund: | | | | | | |
| Treasury Securities | -3,958 | 104,554 | -35,873 | 719,456 | 827,968 | 824,010 |
| Employees Life Insurance Fund | 228 | 664 | 489 | 41,951 | 42,386 | 42,614 |
| Employees and Retired Employees Health Benefits Fund | 407 | 168 | 1,438 | 23,429 | 23,190 | 23,597 |
| Social Security Administration: | | | | | | |
| Federal Old-Age and Survivors Insurance Trust Fund | -7,262 | 32,334 | 38,460 | 2,655,599 | 2,695,194 | 2,687,933 |
| Federal Disability Insurance Trust Fund | -3,451 | -20,035 | -20,835 | 100,791 | 84,208 | 80,757 |
| Independent Agencies: | | | | | | |
| Harry S Truman Memorial Scholarship Trust Fund | -10 | -10 | (**) | 54 | 54 | 44 |
| Japan-United States Friendship Commission | ...... | ...... | ...... | 38 | 38 | 38 |
| Railroad Retirement Board: | | | | | | |
| Treasury Securities | -110 | 142 | 94 | 2,367 | 2,619 | 2,509 |
| Agency Securities | ...... | ...... | 1 | 5 | 5 | 5 |
| Other | -20 | 72 | 355 | 1,355 | 1,446 | 1,426 |
| Total Treasury Securities | -28,554 | 190,489 | 16,941 | 4,335,291 | 4,554,334 | 4,525,780 |
| Total Agency Securities | ...... | ...... | 1 | 5 | 5 | 5 |
| Total Trust Funds | -28,554 | 190,489 | 16,942 | 4,335,297 | 4,554,339 | 4,525,785 |
| Grand Total | -26,103 | 221,855 | 44,521 | 4,757,211 | 5,005,168 | 4,979,066 |

... No Transactions
(**) Less than $500,000

Note: Investments are in Treasury securities unless otherwise noted.
Note: Details may not add to totals due to rounding.

## Table 6. Schedule E-Net Activity, Guaranteed and Direct Loan Financing, May 2014 and Other Periods

[$ millions]

| Classification | Net Transactions (-) denotes net reduction of assets accounts | | | Account Balances Current Fiscal Year | | |
|---|---|---|---|---|---|---|
| | This Month | Fiscal Year to Date | | Beginning of | | Close of This Month |
| | | This Year | Prior Year | This Year | This Month | |
| Guaranteed Loan Financing Activity: | | | | | | |
| Department of Agriculture: | | | | | | |
| Farm Service Agency: | | | | | | |
| Commodity Credit Corporation Export Fund | -3 | -24 | -60 | 332 | 310 | 307 |
| Agricultural Credit Insurance Fund | -1 | -3 | 2 | -168 | -170 | -171 |
| Natural Resource Conservation Demonstration Program: | | | | | | |
| Agricultural Resource Conservation Demonstration Program | ..... | ..... | ..... | (**) | (**) | (**) |
| Rural Housing Service: | | | | | | |
| Rural Community Facility Loans | (**) | -2 | -1 | -57 | -58 | -59 |
| Rural Housing Insurance Fund | 12 | 9 | 129 | -3,047 | -3,050 | -3,038 |
| Rural Business-Cooperative Service: | | | | | | |
| Rural Business and Industry Loans | -3 | -31 | 29 | -492 | -520 | -523 |
| Renewable Energy Guaranteed Loan Account | (**) | -7 | -6 | -40 | -46 | -46 |
| Biorefinery Assistance Loan Account | ..... | (**) | -1 | -44 | -44 | -44 |
| Rural Utilities Service: | | | | | | |
| Rural Water and Waste Disposal Fund | (**) | (**) | (**) | -25 | -25 | -25 |
| Department of Commerce: | | | | | | |
| General Administration: | | | | | | |
| Emergency Oil, Gas, and Steel Account | ..... | ..... | ..... | 5 | 5 | 5 |
| National Oceanic and Atmospheric Administration: | | | | | | |
| Fishing Vessel Obligations | (**) | (**) | (**) | (**) | (**) | ..... |
| Department of Defense-Military Programs | ..... | ..... | (**) | -47 | -47 | -47 |
| Department of Education: | | | | | | |
| Office of Student Financial Assistance: | | | | | | |
| Federal Family Education Loans | -448 | 1,483 | -2,265 | 34,848 | 36,778 | 36,331 |
| Department of Energy: | | | | | | |
| Title 17 Innovative Technology Loans | -4 | -37 | 5 | -169 | -203 | -206 |
| Department of Health and Human Services: | | | | | | |
| Health Resources and Services Administration: | | | | | | |
| Health Center Loans | ..... | (**) | ..... | -3 | -2 | -2 |
| Health Education Assistance Loans | 44 | 42 | 1 | -112 | -113 | -69 |
| Department of Housing and Urban Development: | | | | | | |
| Public and Indian Housing Programs: | | | | | | |
| Indian Housing Loans | (**) | (**) | 7 | -48 | -49 | -48 |
| Native Hawaiian Housing Loans | 1 | 1 | 1 | (**) | (**) | 1 |
| Community Planning and Development: | | | | | | |
| Community Development Loans | ..... | 4 | -1 | -107 | -103 | -103 |
| Housing Programs: | | | | | | |
| FHA-Mutual Mortgage Insurance Loans | 902 | 6,525 | 15,452 | -26,306 | -20,683 | -19,782 |
| FHA-General and Special Risk Fund | 2,522 | 3,182 | 1,492 | -8,219 | -7,559 | -5,037 |
| Home Ownership Preservation Entity Fund | (**) | 1 | (**) | -20 | -19 | -19 |
| Government National Mortgage Association: | | | | | | |
| Guarantees of Mortgaged-Backed Securities | -108 | -1,485 | -1,263 | 4,956 | 3,579 | 3,472 |

## Table 6. Schedule E-Net Activity, Guaranteed and Direct Loan Financing, May 2014 and Other Periods —Continued
[$ millions]

| Classification | Net Transactions (-) denotes net reduction of assets accounts | | | Account Balances Current Fiscal Year | | |
|---|---|---|---|---|---|---|
| | This Month | Fiscal Year to Date | | Beginning of | | Close of |
| | | This Year | Prior Year | This Year | This Month | This Month |
| Guaranteed Loan Financing Activity:—Continued | | | | | | |
| Department of the Interior: | | | | | | |
| Bureau of Indian Affairs | (**) | -1 | (**) | -56 | -57 | -57 |
| Department of Transportation: | | | | | | |
| Office of the Secretary: | | | | | | |
| Minority Business Resource Center Fund | (**) | (**) | (**) | -1 | (**) | (**) |
| Federal Highway Administration: | | | | | | |
| Transportation Infrastructure Finance and Innovation Fund | ...... | ...... | ...... | (**) | (**) | (**) |
| Maritime Administration: | | | | | | |
| Maritime Guaranteed Loan (Title XI) Fund | ...... | -10 | (**) | -194 | -204 | -204 |
| Department of the Treasury: | | | | | | |
| Departmental Offices: | | | | | | |
| Air Transportation Stabilization Fund | ...... | ...... | ...... | (**) | (**) | (**) |
| Troubled Assets Insurance Financing Fund | ...... | ...... | -890 | (**) | (**) | (**) |
| Troubled Asset Relief Program | ...... | 2 | -3 | -15 | -13 | -13 |
| Department of Veterans Affairs: | | | | | | |
| Veterans Benefits Administration: | | | | | | |
| Veterans Housing Benefit Program Fund | -50 | -2,053 | 292 | -5,356 | -7,360 | -7,409 |
| International Assistance Program: | | | | | | |
| Agency for International Development: | | | | | | |
| Ukraine Export Credit Insurance Fund | -194 | -194 | ...... | ...... | ...... | -194 |
| Loan Guarantees to Israel | ...... | ...... | ...... | -1,379 | -1,379 | -1,379 |
| Urban and Environmental Credit Guaranteed Loans | 1 | 2 | 1 | -56 | -55 | -55 |
| Microenterprise and Small Enterprise Development | ...... | ...... | ...... | (**) | (**) | (**) |
| Development Credit Authority Loan Fund | -1 | -5 | -4 | -54 | -58 | -59 |
| Loan Guarantees to Egypt | ...... | ...... | ...... | -458 | -458 | -458 |
| Tunisia Loan Fund | ...... | -122 | ...... | -12 | -134 | -134 |
| Overseas Private Investment Corporation | 11 | -27 | 21 | 125 | 88 | 99 |
| Small Business Administration: | | | | | | |
| Business Loan Fund | -10 | 344 | 732 | -2,156 | -1,802 | -1,812 |
| Independent Agencies: | | | | | | |
| Export-Import Bank of the United States | 575 | 349 | -221 | -1,995 | -2,222 | -1,646 |
| Net Activity, Guaranteed Loan Financing | 3,247 | 7,941 | 13,450 | -10,369 | -5,674 | -2,427 |

## Table 6. Schedule E-Net Activity, Guaranteed and Direct Loan Financing, May 2014 and Other Periods —Continued

[$ millions]

| Classification | Net Transactions (-) denotes net reduction of assets accounts | | | Account Balances Current Fiscal Year | | |
|---|---|---|---|---|---|---|
| | This Month | Fiscal Year to Date | | Beginning of | | Close of |
| | | This Year | Prior Year | This Year | This Month | This Month |
| **Direct Loan Financing Activity:** | | | | | | |
| Department of Agriculture: | | | | | | |
| Farm Service Agency: | | | | | | |
| Agricultural Credit Insurance Fund | 131 | -48 | -328 | 6,949 | 6,770 | 6,902 |
| Farm Storage Facility Loans | 3 | 38 | -3 | 742 | 777 | 780 |
| Apple Loans Fund | ...... | (**) | (**) | (**) | (**) | (**) |
| Emergency Boll Weevil Loan Fund | ...... | ...... | ...... | 3 | 3 | 3 |
| Rural Housing Service: | | | | | | |
| Rural Community Facility Loans Fund | 33 | 117 | 267 | 4,577 | 4,661 | 4,694 |
| Rural Housing Insurance Fund | -48 | -389 | -382 | 15,356 | 15,015 | 14,967 |
| Multifamily Housing Revitalization Loan Account | 1 | 3 | 14 | 197 | 200 | 200 |
| Rural Business-Cooperative Service: | | | | | | |
| Rural Business and Industry Loan Fund | (**) | -1 | -3 | 45 | 44 | 44 |
| Rural Development Loan Fund | -1 | -12 | -12 | 298 | 287 | 286 |
| Rural Economic Development Loan Fund | 2 | 17 | 7 | 111 | 125 | 127 |
| Rural Microenterprise Investment Loans | (**) | 2 | 3 | 17 | 19 | 19 |
| Rural Utilities Service: | | | | | | |
| Rural Water and Waste Disposal Loans | 6 | -66 | -247 | 10,199 | 10,126 | 10,133 |
| Rural Electrification and Telecommunications Fund | 790 | 1,484 | 1,402 | 48,457 | 49,150 | 49,941 |
| Rural Telephone Bank | -6 | -37 | -47 | 293 | 262 | 257 |
| Distance Learning and Telemedicine Program | 1 | 25 | 100 | 1,145 | 1,169 | 1,170 |
| Rural Development Insurance Fund | ...... | ...... | ...... | 1,065 | 1,065 | 1,065 |
| Foreign Agricultural Service: | | | | | | |
| P.L. 480 Direct Loan Fund | -76 | -150 | -77 | 783 | 709 | 633 |
| International Debt Reduction | -1 | -6 | -9 | 5 | 1 | -1 |
| Department of Commerce: | | | | | | |
| National Oceanic and Atmospheric Administration: | | | | | | |
| Fisheries Finance | -11 | -21 | -20 | 525 | 514 | 503 |
| Department of Defense-Military Programs | -4 | 50 | 143 | 1,173 | 1,227 | 1,223 |
| Department of Education: | | | | | | |
| Office of Postsecondary Education: | | | | | | |
| College Housing and Academic Facilities Loans | ...... | -1 | -2 | 5 | 4 | 4 |
| Historically Black College and University Capital | | | | | | |
| Financing Fund | 12 | 68 | 98 | 939 | 996 | 1,007 |
| Office of Student Financial Assistance: | | | | | | |
| Federal Direct Student Loans | 2,910 | 65,061 | 78,463 | 674,580 | 736,731 | 739,641 |
| Teach Grant Loans | 2 | 41 | 60 | 453 | 491 | 494 |
| Temporary Student Loan Purchase Authority | -820 | -6,888 | -6,791 | 107,415 | 101,347 | 100,527 |
| Department of Energy: | | | | | | |
| Advanced Technology Vehicles Manufacturing Loans | ...... | -310 | 142 | 5,651 | 5,342 | 5,342 |
| Title 17 Innovative Technology Loans | 2 | 1,376 | 2,120 | 6,726 | 8,100 | 8,102 |
| Department of Health and Human Services: | | | | | | |
| Consumer Operated and Oriented Plan | 19 | 227 | 210 | 417 | 626 | 644 |
| Consumer Operated and Oriented Plan Prog Contingency Fund | ...... | 19 | ...... | 1 | 20 | 20 |
| Department of Homeland Security: | | | | | | |
| Disaster Assistance Loan Fund | -6 | 12 | -7 | 39 | 57 | 52 |
| Department of Housing and Urban Development: | | | | | | |
| Housing Programs: | | | | | | |
| Emergency Homeowners' Relief Fund | (**) | -1 | (**) | 2 | 1 | 1 |
| FHA-Mutual Mortgage Insurance Fund | ...... | (**) | (**) | -5 | -5 | -5 |
| FHA-General and Special Risk Fund | ...... | ...... | ...... | (**) | (**) | (**) |
| Green Retrofit Program for Multifamily Housing Fund | -1 | -4 | -3 | 6 | 3 | 2 |

## Table 6. Schedule E-Net Activity, Guaranteed and Direct Loan Financing, May 2014 and Other Periods —Continued

[$ millions]

| Classification | Net Transactions (-) denotes net reduction of assets accounts | | | Account Balances Current Fiscal Year | | |
|---|---|---|---|---|---|---|
| | This Month | Fiscal Year to Date | | Beginning of | | Close of |
| | | This Year | Prior Year | This Year | This Month | This Month |
| Direct Loan Financing Activity:—Continued | | | | | | |
| Department of the Interior: | | | | | | |
| Bureau of Reclamation | ..... | -3 | -3 | 36 | 33 | 33 |
| Bureau of Indian Affairs | (**) | -1 | -1 | 4 | 3 | 3 |
| Assistance to American Samoa Loan Fund | ..... | -1 | -1 | 9 | 8 | 8 |
| Department of State: | | | | | | |
| Administration of Foreign Affairs: | | | | | | |
| Repatriation Loans | (**) | -1 | -1 | 1 | (**) | (**) |
| Department of Transportation: | | | | | | |
| Federal Highway Administration: | | | | | | |
| Transportation Infrastructure Finance and Innovation Fund | 26 | 781 | 512 | 5,677 | 6,432 | 6,458 |
| Tiger Tifia Loan Fund | 4 | 17 | ..... | 401 | 414 | 418 |
| Federal Railroad Administration: | | | | | | |
| Railroad Rehabilitation and Improvement Loan Fund | 7 | 2 | 47 | 810 | 805 | 812 |
| Department of the Treasury: | | | | | | |
| Departmental Offices: | | | | | | |
| Community Development Financial Institutions Fund | 7 | 13 | (**) | 38 | 44 | 51 |
| GSE Mortgage-Backed Securities Purchase Program | ..... | ..... | ..... | 4,613 | 4,613 | 4,613 |
| Temporary Credit and Liquidity Program | -66 | -680 | -3,684 | 8,458 | 7,844 | 7,779 |
| Troubled Asset Relief Program | -227 | -7,820 | -15,459 | 9,735 | 2,142 | 1,915 |
| Small Business Lending Program | -40 | -360 | -316 | 3,639 | 3,318 | 3,279 |
| Bureau of the Fiscal Service: | | | | | | |
| Financial Management Service | ..... | ..... | ..... | (**) | (**) | (**) |
| Department of Veterans Affairs: | | | | | | |
| Veterans Benefits Administration: | | | | | | |
| Veterans Housing Benefit Program Fund | -7 | -38 | -39 | 570 | 539 | 532 |
| Native American Veteran Housing Fund | -1 | -1 | 7 | 62 | 63 | 62 |
| Transitional Housing Loans | (**) | (**) | (**) | (**) | (**) | (**) |
| Vocational Rehabilitation Loan Fund | (**) | (**) | (**) | 1 | 1 | 1 |
| Environmental Protection Agency: | | | | | | |
| Abatement, Control, and Compliance Loan Program | ..... | (**) | (**) | (**) | (**) | (**) |
| International Assistance Program: | | | | | | |
| International Security Assistance: | | | | | | |
| Foreign Military Loan Program | ..... | ..... | ..... | -27 | -27 | -27 |
| Military Debt Reduction | ..... | ..... | ..... | 36 | 36 | 36 |
| Agency for International Development: | | | | | | |
| International Debt Reduction | ..... | -12 | -25 | 116 | 104 | 104 |
| Overseas Private Investment Corporation | 1 | -34 | 95 | 1,359 | 1,324 | 1,325 |
| International Monetary Programs | -6 | -9 | -8 | -60 | -62 | -68 |
| Small Business Administration: | | | | | | |
| Business Loan Fund | -1 | 18 | 7 | 124 | 142 | 142 |
| Disaster Loan Fund | -54 | -312 | -159 | 5,858 | 5,601 | 5,546 |
| Independent Agencies: | | | | | | |
| Export-Import Bank of the United States | -577 | 987 | 3,842 | 17,086 | 18,651 | 18,073 |
| Federal Communications Commission: | | | | | | |
| Spectrum Auction Loan Fund | (**) | 3 | -2 | -6 | -3 | -3 |
| Net Activity, Direct Loan Financing | 2,006 | 53,156 | 59,913 | 946,711 | 997,861 | 999,867 |

Note: Federal credit programs provide benefits to the public in the form of direct loans and loan guarantees. This table reflects cash transactions and balances of the nonbudgetary financing fund accounts that result from the disbursement of loans, collection of fees, repayment of principle, sale of collateral, interest, and subsidy received from the credit program accounts at net present value in accordance with the Credit Reform Act of 1990. Unreimbursed costs such as administrative expenses and subsidy payments are reported on a cash basis and included within each program's budgetary totals in Table 5.

... No Transactions
(**) Less than $500,000
Note: Details may not add to totals due to rounding.

## Table 7. Receipts and Outlays of the U.S. Government by Month, Fiscal Year 2014

[$ millions]

| Classification | Oct. | Nov. | Dec. | Jan. | Feb. | March | April | May | June | July | Aug. | Sept. | Fiscal Year to Date | Comparable Period Prior F.Y. |
|---|---|---|---|---|---|---|---|---|---|---|---|---|---|---|
| **Receipts:** | | | | | | | | | | | | | | |
| Individual Income Taxes | 99,106 | 82,711 | 124,608 | 169,388 | 37,956 | 71,145 | 238,164 | 79,945 | | | | | 903,024 | 873,862 |
| Corporation Income Taxes | 6,475 | 498 | 62,287 | 8,147 | 8,015 | 32,133 | 39,253 | 8,031 | | | | | 164,840 | 142,632 |
| Social Insurance and Retirement Receipts: | | | | | | | | | | | | | | |
| Employment and General Retirement | 67,580 | 72,817 | 75,820 | 90,888 | 73,864 | 89,569 | 102,538 | 75,668 | | | | | 648,743 | 581,795 |
| Unemployment Insurance | 3,340 | 4,590 | 472 | 5,497 | 3,694 | 473 | 9,574 | 15,591 | | | | | 43,231 | 45,605 |
| Other Retirement | 293 | 273 | 273 | 266 | 319 | 308 | 252 | 311 | | | | | 2,294 | 2,398 |
| Excise Taxes | 5,852 | 6,938 | 6,418 | 6,540 | 6,238 | 6,375 | 7,505 | 5,697 | | | | | 51,563 | 52,650 |
| Estate and Gift Taxes | 1,772 | 2,109 | 1,406 | 1,248 | 1,062 | 1,152 | 2,402 | 1,432 | | | | | 12,582 | 13,720 |
| Customs Duties | 3,166 | 2,848 | 2,833 | 3,000 | 2,484 | 2,475 | 2,886 | 2,434 | | | | | 22,125 | 20,568 |
| Miscellaneous Receipts | 11,344 | 9,668 | 9,105 | 11,024 | 10,718 | 12,216 | 11,662 | 10,781 | | | | | 86,517 | 67,287 |
| Total--Receipts This Year | 198,927 | 182,453 | 283,221 | 295,997 | 144,349 | 215,846 | 414,237 | 199,889 | | | | | 1,934,919 | ....... |
| (On-Budget) | 148,871 | 128,657 | 228,231 | 226,228 | 86,974 | 145,924 | 335,529 | 140,789 | | | | | 1,441,203 | ....... |
| (Off-Budget) | 50,056 | 53,796 | 54,990 | 69,769 | 57,375 | 69,922 | 78,708 | 59,100 | | | | | 493,716 | ....... |
| *Total--Receipts Prior Year* | *184,316* | *161,730* | *269,508* | *272,225* | *122,815* | *186,018* | *406,723* | *197,182* | | | | | ...... | *1,800,515* |
| *(On Budget)* | *144,166* | *118,561* | *230,049* | *207,810* | *67,807* | *120,570* | *332,553* | *139,762* | | | | | ...... | *1,361,277* |
| *(Off Budget)* | *40,150* | *43,169* | *39,459* | *64,415* | *55,008* | *65,448* | *74,170* | *57,420* | | | | | ...... | *439,239* |
| **Outlays:** | | | | | | | | | | | | | | |
| Legislative Branch | 358 | 344 | 329 | 340 | 311 | 374 | 323 | 337 | | | | | 2,716 | 2,976 |
| Judicial Branch | 573 | 533 | 532 | 677 | 501 | 604 | 542 | 534 | | | | | 4,496 | 4,762 |
| Department of Agriculture: | | | | | | | | | | | | | | |
| Commodity Credit Corporation and Foreign Agricultural Service | 5,623 | 2,493 | 1,219 | 882 | 497 | -515 | -88 | 115 | | | | | 10,228 | 10,719 |
| Other | 12,287 | 11,367 | 12,663 | 11,542 | 10,553 | 11,497 | 10,656 | 9,903 | | | | | 90,467 | 103,664 |
| Department of Commerce | 512 | 625 | 669 | 615 | 614 | 816 | 668 | 623 | | | | | 5,144 | 6,160 |
| Department of Defense: | | | | | | | | | | | | | | |
| Military Programs: | | | | | | | | | | | | | | |
| Military Personnel | 24,883 | 16,043 | 11,041 | 10,843 | 11,017 | 6,764 | 10,763 | 16,299 | | | | | 107,652 | 109,324 |
| Operation and Maintenance | 19,727 | 18,718 | 19,947 | 18,949 | 20,098 | 20,518 | 20,847 | 21,030 | | | | | 159,835 | 175,476 |
| International Reconstruction and Other Assistance | (**) | 1 | ...... | ...... | (**) | (**) | (**) | (**) | | | | | 1 | 1 |
| Procurement | 7,111 | 7,301 | 10,524 | 14,086 | 7,279 | 10,071 | 9,785 | 7,029 | | | | | 73,186 | 76,153 |
| Research, Development, Test, and Evaluation | 4,437 | 4,569 | 6,587 | 4,030 | 5,470 | 6,112 | 5,943 | 4,678 | | | | | 41,825 | 44,192 |
| Military Construction | 842 | 868 | 807 | 899 | 633 | 744 | 836 | 732 | | | | | 6,362 | 8,107 |
| Family Housing | 104 | 118 | 113 | 69 | 118 | -210 | 124 | 395 | | | | | 830 | 1,349 |
| Revolving and Management Funds | 203 | 197 | 885 | 1,780 | -320 | 543 | -712 | -525 | | | | | 2,051 | 2,283 |
| Other | 84 | -605 | -14 | -185 | 66 | 346 | -386 | -748 | | | | | -1,442 | -1,494 |
| Total Military Programs | 57,391 | 47,209 | 49,890 | 50,472 | 44,361 | 44,888 | 47,200 | 48,891 | | | | | 390,300 | 415,390 |
| Department of Education | 2,857 | 5,503 | 5,620 | 760 | 4,760 | 6,161 | 5,175 | 5,164 | | | | | 36,000 | 36,294 |
| Department of Energy | 2,331 | 1,809 | 2,192 | 1,783 | 1,644 | 2,049 | 2,023 | 1,710 | | | | | 15,543 | 16,449 |
| Department of Health and Human Services: | | | | | | | | | | | | | | |
| National Institutes of Health | 2,169 | 2,719 | 2,406 | 2,239 | 2,322 | 2,629 | 2,929 | 2,471 | | | | | 19,884 | 20,495 |
| Centers for Medicare and Medicaid Services: | | | | | | | | | | | | | | |
| Grants to States for Medicaid | 24,594 | 20,620 | 23,002 | 24,000 | 24,274 | 23,847 | 24,904 | 25,709 | | | | | 190,950 | 176,575 |
| Federal Hospital Ins. Trust Fund | 21,717 | 26,638 | 16,432 | 28,326 | 22,512 | 15,619 | 22,470 | 29,555 | | | | | 183,269 | 184,499 |
| Federal Supp. Med. Ins. Trust Fund | 22,031 | 37,847 | 15,410 | 41,359 | 23,790 | 14,750 | 28,333 | 40,110 | | | | | 223,631 | 214,492 |
| Other | 24,908 | 27,478 | 17,645 | 28,403 | 19,113 | 18,924 | 29,857 | 25,028 | | | | | 191,356 | 171,724 |
| Administration for Children and Families | 3,647 | 3,955 | 4,287 | 4,322 | 3,805 | 4,181 | 4,277 | 3,981 | | | | | 32,454 | 33,603 |
| Other | -22,434 | -30,459 | -20,473 | -35,463 | -23,585 | -20,302 | -33,417 | -31,422 | | | | | -217,555 | -194,955 |
| Department of Homeland Security | 3,592 | 3,598 | 3,674 | 3,573 | 3,045 | 4,022 | 3,218 | 3,074 | | | | | 27,798 | 41,206 |
| Department of Housing and Urban Development | 2,916 | 3,383 | 3,226 | 3,255 | 3,301 | 6,091 | 3,197 | 1,042 | | | | | 26,410 | 21,339 |
| Department of the Interior | 1,194 | 959 | 435 | 834 | 667 | 1,061 | 1,256 | 788 | | | | | 7,193 | 5,117 |
| Department of Justice | 2,830 | 2,503 | 69 | 2,316 | 1,551 | 3,305 | 2,610 | 1,975 | | | | | 17,158 | 20,429 |
| Department of Labor: | | | | | | | | | | | | | | |
| Unemployment Trust Fund | 5,122 | 4,627 | 5,154 | 4,794 | 4,057 | 3,755 | 3,876 | 3,235 | | | | | 34,620 | 51,662 |
| Other | -1,235 | 1,125 | 1,735 | 1,269 | 1,061 | 746 | 8 | 1,141 | | | | | 5,850 | 5,591 |
| Department of State | 2,218 | 2,488 | 2,362 | 1,689 | 1,424 | 2,366 | 3,000 | 1,650 | | | | | 17,196 | 16,088 |
| Department of Transportation: | | | | | | | | | | | | | | |
| Highway Trust Fund | 4,104 | 3,535 | 3,492 | 2,437 | 2,205 | 2,727 | 3,079 | 2,727 | | | | | 24,305 | 23,723 |
| Other | 2,799 | 3,007 | 2,933 | 2,248 | 2,656 | 2,426 | 3,143 | 2,249 | | | | | 21,461 | 22,809 |
| Department of the Treasury: | | | | | | | | | | | | | | |
| Interest on Treasury Debt Securities (Gross) | 15,799 | 22,327 | 87,712 | 19,499 | 21,266 | 26,270 | 31,100 | 32,081 | | | | | 256,054 | 252,230 |
| Other | 2,248 | 2,330 | -36,745 | 2,995 | 63,438 | -8,958 | 11,809 | 6,483 | | | | | 43,600 | 81,839 |

[$ millions]

| Classification | Oct. | Nov. | Dec. | Jan. | Feb. | March | April | May | June | July | Aug. | Sept. | Fiscal Year to Date | Comparable Period Prior F.Y. |
|---|---|---|---|---|---|---|---|---|---|---|---|---|---|---|
| **Outlays:—Continued** | | | | | | | | | | | | | | |
| Department of Veterans Affairs: | | | | | | | | | | | | | | |
| Compensation and Pensions | 5,719 | 10,576 | 5,697 | 5,613 | 5,982 | 740 | 5,850 | 11,083 | | | | | 51,261 | 46,856 |
| National Service Life | 83 | 64 | 65 | 76 | 73 | 89 | 94 | 79 | | | | | 622 | 651 |
| Other | 6,324 | 6,314 | 5,884 | 7,511 | 5,928 | 7,402 | 7,000 | 6,434 | | | | | 52,798 | 47,691 |
| Corps of Engineers | 725 | 529 | 513 | 474 | 455 | 545 | 524 | 622 | | | | | 4,387 | 4,446 |
| Other Defense Civil Programs | 5,403 | 9,112 | 5,986 | 5,347 | 4,844 | 460 | 3,152 | 8,398 | | | | | 42,701 | 41,791 |
| Environmental Protection | 790 | 730 | 613 | 823 | 601 | 626 | 774 | 624 | | | | | 5,581 | 6,607 |
| Executive Office of the President | 23 | 34 | 29 | 39 | 29 | 27 | 34 | 30 | | | | | 244 | 252 |
| General Services Administration | 76 | -21 | -158 | 64 | -134 | -140 | 127 | 80 | | | | | -107 | -118 |
| International Assistance Program: | | | | | | | | | | | | | | |
| International Security Assistance | 1,212 | 851 | 1,365 | 634 | 2,613 | 541 | 454 | 619 | | | | | 8,289 | 7,182 |
| Multilateral Assistance | 3 | 249 | 158 | 20 | 1 | 21 | 153 | 322 | | | | | 927 | 787 |
| Agency for International Development | 469 | 365 | 399 | 537 | 671 | 231 | 159 | 731 | | | | | 3,564 | 3,668 |
| Other | -259 | -691 | 539 | -61 | 13 | 207 | -27 | 15 | | | | | -264 | 972 |
| National Aeronautics and Space Administration | 968 | 1,617 | 1,880 | 1,160 | 1,252 | 1,593 | 1,255 | 1,344 | | | | | 11,069 | 11,044 |
| National Science Foundation | 504 | 653 | 480 | 486 | 510 | 498 | 534 | 520 | | | | | 4,184 | 4,483 |
| Office of Personnel Management | 7,662 | 7,216 | 6,652 | 7,766 | 6,857 | 7,538 | 8,206 | 6,929 | | | | | 58,826 | 55,920 |
| Small Business Administration | 89 | 96 | 81 | 76 | -709 | 84 | 77 | 86 | | | | | -121 | 57 |
| Social Security Administration: | | | | | | | | | | | | | | |
| Federal Old-Age and Survivors Ins. Trust Fund (Off-Budget) | 56,690 | 57,026 | 57,579 | 58,152 | 58,229 | 58,718 | 58,867 | 59,012 | | | | | 464,274 | 440,631 |
| Federal Disability Ins. Trust Fund (Off-Budget) | 11,755 | 12,003 | 11,718 | 11,966 | 11,923 | 12,205 | 12,184 | 12,123 | | | | | 95,877 | 94,418 |
| Other | 4,475 | 8,799 | 4,761 | 4,631 | 4,607 | 98 | 4,644 | 9,156 | | | | | 41,171 | 40,120 |
| Independent Agencies: | | | | | | | | | | | | | | |
| Fed. Deposit Ins. Corp: | | | | | | | | | | | | | | |
| Deposit Insurance Fund | -58 | -676 | -3,032 | 375 | -1,143 | -1,904 | 182 | -435 | | | | | -6,692 | -45 |
| FSLIC Resolution Fund | (**) | (**) | -2 | 1 | (**) | (**) | (**) | (**) | | | | | -1 | 180 |
| Postal Service: | | | | | | | | | | | | | | |
| Off-Budget: | | | | | | | | | | | | | | |
| Public Enterprise Funds | 429 | -805 | -1,105 | 436 | -456 | -51 | -730 | -269 | | | | | -2,551 | -2,588 |
| Other | 4 | 71 | ...... | 10 | 171 | (**) | ...... | ...... | | | | | 256 | 255 |
| Other | 78 | ...... | (**) | (**) | (**) | (**) | (**) | (**) | | | | | 78 | 78 |
| Tennessee Valley Authority | 3 | -459 | -186 | -250 | -204 | -89 | -44 | -126 | | | | | -1,355 | 234 |
| Other Independent Agencies | 994 | 1,955 | 960 | 2,698 | 2,831 | 1,809 | 2,150 | 2,643 | | | | | 16,040 | 20,786 |
| Undistributed Offsetting Receipts: | | | | | | | | | | | | | | |
| Employer Share, Employee Retirement | -19,361 | -5,246 | -5,240 | -5,636 | -5,240 | -5,580 | -5,047 | -5,758 | | | | | -57,108 | -59,057 |
| Interest Received by Trust Funds | 5,134 | -1,150 | -70,528 | -1,337 | -1,487 | -1,725 | -4,762 | -3,340 | | | | | -79,194 | -76,962 |
| Rents and Royalties on Outer Continental Shelf Lands | -571 | -93 | -980 | -531 | -481 | -541 | -575 | -213 | | | | | -3,986 | -5,790 |
| Sale of Major Assets | ...... | ...... | ...... | ...... | ...... | ...... | ...... | ...... | | | | | ...... | -2,588 |
| Other | (**) | (**) | (**) | ...... | ...... | ...... | ...... | (**) | | | | | (**) | (**) |
| **Totals This Year:** | | | | | | | | | | | | | | |
| Total Outlays | 289,511 | 317,679 | 230,001 | 306,247 | 337,880 | 252,739 | 307,383 | 329,860 | | | | | 2,371,301 | ...... |
| (On-Budget) | 225,419 | 250,867 | 212,435 | 244,403 | 269,430 | 183,530 | 245,856 | 260,468 | | | | | 1,892,407 | ...... |
| (Off-Budget) | 64,093 | 66,813 | 17,566 | 61,844 | 68,450 | 69,208 | 61,527 | 69,392 | | | | | 478,894 | ...... |
| Total-Surplus (+) or Deficit (-) | -90,584 | -135,226 | +53,220 | -10,250 | -193,532 | -36,893 | +106,853 | -129,971 | | | | | -436,382 | ...... |
| (On-Budget) | -76,547 | -122,210 | +15,796 | -18,174 | -182,457 | -37,606 | +89,673 | -119,679 | | | | | -451,204 | ...... |
| (Off-Budget) | -14,037 | -13,017 | +37,424 | +7,925 | -11,075 | +713 | +17,181 | -10,292 | | | | | +14,822 | ...... |
| Total Borrowing from the Public | 204,141 | 93,153 | 73,643 | -48,518 | 183,562 | 126,952 | -115,417 | 34,692 | | | | | 552,208 | 631,896 |
| *Total-Outlays Prior Year* | *304,311* | *333,841* | *270,699* | *269,340* | *326,354* | *292,548* | *293,834* | *335,914* | | | | | ...... | *2,426,840* |
| *(On-Budget)* | *255,939* | *278,998* | *267,740* | *212,015* | *260,700* | *226,200* | *236,743* | *269,499* | | | | | ...... | *2,007,834* |
| *(Off-Budget)* | *48,372* | *54,844* | *2,959* | *57,324* | *65,653* | *66,348* | *57,091* | *66,415* | | | | | ...... | *419,006* |
| *Total-Surplus (+) or Deficit (-) Prior Year* | *-119,995* | *-172,112* | *-1,191* | *+2,886* | *-203,539* | *-106,530* | *+112,889* | *-138,732* | | | | | ...... | *-626,325* |
| *(On-Budget)* | *-111,774* | *-160,437* | *-37,691* | *-4,205* | *-192,894* | *-105,630* | *+95,810* | *-129,737* | | | | | ...... | *-646,558* |
| *(Off-Budget)* | *-8,222* | *-11,675* | *+36,500* | *+7,091* | *-10,645* | *-900* | *+17,079* | *-8,995* | | | | | ...... | *+20,233* |

... No Transactions
(**) Less than $500,000

Note: Details may not add to totals due to rounding.

## Table 8. Trust Fund Impact on Budget Results and Investment Holdings as of May 31, 2014
[$ millions]

| Classification | This Month | | | Fiscal Year to Date | | | Securities Held as Investments Current Fiscal Year | | |
| --- | --- | --- | --- | --- | --- | --- | --- | --- | --- |
| | | | | | | | Beginning of | | Close of This Month |
| | Receipts | Outlays | Excess | Receipts | Outlays | Excess | This Year | This Month | |
| **Trust Receipts, Outlays, and Investments Held:** | | | | | | | | | |
| Airport and Airway | 1,234 | 1,081 | 152 | 8,264 | 8,563 | -299 | 11,808 | 11,867 | 11,862 |
| Black Lung Disability | 48 | 18 | 30 | 368 | 149 | 219 | ...... | ...... | ...... |
| Federal Disability Insurance | 8,813 | 12,123 | -3,310 | 76,010 | 95,877 | -19,866 | 100,791 | 84,208 | 80,757 |
| Federal Employees Life and Health | ...... | -634 | 634 | ...... | -1,058 | 1,058 | 65,380 | 65,576 | 66,211 |
| Federal Employees Retirement | 2,772 | 6,693 | -3,921 | 35,175 | 53,594 | -18,419 | 737,855 | 846,533 | 842,616 |
| Federal Hospital Insurance | 18,781 | 29,655 | -10,874 | 177,488 | 184,108 | -6,620 | 206,010 | 210,263 | 199,291 |
| Federal Old-Age and Survivors Insurance | 51,761 | 59,012 | -7,251 | 496,668 | 464,274 | 32,393 | 2,655,599 | 2,695,194 | 2,687,933 |
| Federal Supplementary Medical Insurance | 31,532 | 40,110 | -8,578 | 221,939 | 223,628 | -1,689 | 67,385 | 76,596 | 68,131 |
| Hazardous Substance Superfund | 5 | 133 | -128 | 1,030 | 494 | 535 | 3,187 | 3,818 | 3,750 |
| Highways | 3,371 | 3,666 | -295 | 35,305 | 30,579 | 4,726 | 1,957 | 9,852 | 9,966 |
| Military Advances | 2,257 | 2,110 | 146 | 18,526 | 17,498 | 1,028 | ...... | ...... | ...... |
| Military Retirement | 4,726 | 8,866 | -4,140 | 98,765 | 41,037 | 57,728 | 421,327 | 487,544 | 483,111 |
| Railroad Retirement | 730 | 1,107 | -377 | 8,199 | 8,842 | -643 | 2,372 | 2,625 | 2,515 |
| Unemployment | 15,727 | 3,244 | 12,483 | 49,418 | 34,690 | 14,727 | 29,478 | 27,511 | 37,016 |
| Veterans Life Insurance | 5 | 96 | -91 | 165 | 696 | -531 | 8,180 | 7,739 | 7,651 |
| All Other Trust | 619 | 506 | 112 | 4,992 | 3,799 | 1,193 | 23,968 | 25,014 | 24,976 |
| **Total Trust Fund Receipts and Outlays and Investments Held from Table 6-D** | 142,379 | 167,787 | -25,408 | 1,232,310 | 1,166,770 | 65,540 | 4,335,297 | 4,554,339 | 4,525,785 |
| Less: Interfund Transactions | 45,793 | 45,793 | ...... | 502,016 | 502,016 | ...... | | | |
| Trust Fund Receipts and Outlays on the Basis of Tables 4 & 5 | 96,586 | 121,994 | -25,408 | 730,294 | 664,754 | 65,540 | | | |
| **Total Federal Fund Receipts and Outlays** | 103,360 | 207,923 | -104,563 | 1,205,124 | 1,707,045 | -501,922 | | | |
| Less: Interfund Transactions | 57 | 57 | ...... | 499 | 499 | ...... | | | |
| Federal Fund Receipts and Outlays on the Basis of Table 4 & 5 | 103,303 | 207,866 | -104,563 | 1,204,624 | 1,706,546 | -501,922 | | | |
| **Net Budget Receipts & Outlays** | 199,889 | 329,860 | -129,971 | 1,934,919 | 2,371,301 | -436,382 | | | |

Note: Interfund receipts and outlays are transactions between Federal funds and trust funds such as Federal payments and contributions, and interest and profits on investments in Federal securities. They have no net effect on overall budget receipts and outlays since the receipt side of such transactions is offset against budget outlays. In this table, Interfund receipts are shown as an adjustment to arrive at total receipts and outlays of trust funds respectively.

... No Transactions

Note: Details may not add to totals due to rounding.

## Table 9. Summary of Receipts by Source, and Outlays by Function of the U.S. Government, May 2014 and Other Periods
[$ millions]

| Classification | This Month | Fiscal Year to Date | Comparable Period Prior Fiscal Year |
| --- | --- | --- | --- |
| **Receipts** | | | |
| Individual Income Taxes | 79,945 | 903,024 | 873,862 |
| Corporation Income Taxes | 8,031 | 164,840 | 142,632 |
| Social Insurance and Retirement Receipts: | | | |
| Employment and General Retirement | 75,668 | 648,743 | 581,795 |
| Unemployment Insurance | 15,591 | 43,231 | 45,605 |
| Other Retirement | 311 | 2,294 | 2,398 |
| Excise Taxes | 5,697 | 51,563 | 52,650 |
| Estate and Gift Taxes | 1,432 | 12,582 | 13,720 |
| Customs Duties | 2,434 | 22,125 | 20,568 |
| Miscellaneous Receipts | 10,781 | 86,517 | 67,287 |
| Total | 199,889 | 1,934,919 | 1,800,515 |
| **Net Outlays** | | | |
| National Defense | 50,915 | 408,630 | 434,207 |
| International Affairs | 4,034 | 30,429 | 28,948 |
| General Science, Space, and Technology | 2,218 | 18,192 | 18,589 |
| Energy | 140 | 2,006 | 7,194 |
| Natural Resources and Environment | 2,581 | 22,476 | 24,536 |
| Agriculture | 651 | 23,120 | 29,572 |
| Commerce and Housing Credit | -2,556 | -74,084 | -27,392 |
| Transportation | 6,333 | 56,271 | 57,371 |
| Community and Regional Development | 1,684 | 14,081 | 24,377 |
| Education, Training, Employment and Social Services | 7,557 | 57,103 | 58,195 |
| Health | 34,734 | 261,142 | 238,237 |
| Medicare | 59,966 | 349,467 | 346,853 |
| Income Security | 46,649 | 384,106 | 399,562 |
| Social Security | 71,131 | 560,142 | 535,025 |
| Veterans Benefits and Services | 17,631 | 105,021 | 95,596 |
| Administration of Justice | 3,755 | 33,717 | 36,435 |
| General Government | 1,281 | 11,440 | 17,555 |
| Net Interest | 27,127 | 169,136 | 169,416 |
| Undistributed Offsetting Receipts | -5,971 | -61,094 | -67,435 |
| Total | 329,860 | 2,371,301 | 2,426,840 |

Note: Details may not add to totals due to rounding.

# Explanatory Notes

### 1. Flow of Data into Monthly Treasury Statement

The Monthly Treasury Statement (MTS) is assembled from data in the central accounting system. The major sources of data include monthly accounting reports by Federal entities and disbursing officers, and daily reports from the Federal Reserve banks. These reports detail accounting transactions affecting receipts and outlays of the Federal Government and off-budget Federal entities, and their related effect on the assets and liabilities of the U.S. Government. Information is presented in the MTS on a modified cash basis.

### 2. Notes on Receipts

Receipts included in the report are classified into the following major categories: (1) budget receipts and (2) offsetting collections (also called applicable receipts). Budget receipts are collections from the public that result from the exercise of the Government's sovereign or governmental powers, excluding receipts offset against outlays. These collections, also called governmental receipts, consist mainly of tax receipts (including social insurance taxes), receipts from court fines, certain licenses, and deposits of earnings by the Federal Reserve System. Refunds of receipts are treated as deductions from gross receipts.

Offsetting collections are from other Government accounts or the public that are of a business-type or market-oriented nature. They are classified into two major categories: (1) offsetting collections credited to appropriations or fund accounts, and (2) offsetting receipts (i.e., amounts deposited in receipt accounts). Collections credited to appropriation or fund accounts normally can be used without appropriation action by Congress. These occur in two instances: (1) when authorized by law, amounts collected for materials or services are treated as reimbursements to appropriations and (2) in the three types of revolving funds (public enterprise, intra governmental, and trust); collections are netted against spending, and outlays are reported as the net amount.

Offsetting receipts in receipt accounts cannot be used without being appropriated. They are subdivided into two categories: (1) proprietary receipts - these collections are from the public and they are offset against outlays by agency and by function, and (2) intra governmental funds - these are payments into receipt accounts from Governmental appropriation or fund accounts. The transactions may be intrabudgetary when the payment and receipt both occur within the budget or from receipts from off-budget Federal entities in those cases where payment is made by a Federal entity whose budget authority and outlays are excluded from the budget totals.

Intrabudgetary transactions are subdivided into three categories: (1) interfund transactions, where the payments are from one fund group (either Federal funds or trust funds) to a receipt account in the other fund group; (2) Federal intrafund transactions, where the payments and receipts both occur within the Federal fund group; and (3) trust intrafund transactions, where the payments and receipts both occur within the trust fund group.

Offsetting receipts are generally deducted from budget authority and outlays by function, by subfunction, or by agency. There are four types of receipts, however, that are deducted from budget totals as undistributed offsetting receipts. They are: (1) agencies' payments (including payments by off-budget Federal entities) as employers into employees retirement funds, (2) interest received by trust funds, (3) rents and royalties on the Outer Continental Shelf lands, and (4) other interest (i.e., interest collected on Outer Continental Shelf money in deposit funds when such money is transferred into the budget).

### 3. Notes on Outlays

Outlays are generally accounted for on the basis of checks issued, electronic funds transferred, or cash payments made. Certain outlays do not require issuance of cash or checks. An example is charges made against appropriations for that part of employees' salaries withheld for taxes or savings bond allotments - these are counted as payments to the employee and credits for whatever purpose the money was withheld. Outlays are stated net of offsetting collections (including receipts of revolving and management funds) and of refunds. Interest on the public debt (public issues) is recognized on the accrual basis. Federal credit programs subject to the Federal Credit Reform Act of 1990 use the cash basis of accounting and are divided into two components. The portion of the credit activities that involve a cost to the Government (mainly subsidies) is included within the budget program accounts. The remaining portion of the credit activities are in non-budget financing accounts. Outlays of off-budget Federal entities are excluded by law from budget totals. However, they are shown separately and combined with the on-budget outlays to display total Federal outlays.

### 4. Processing

The data on payments and collections are reported by account symbol into the central accounting system. In turn, the data are extracted from this system for use in the preparation of the MTS.

There are two major checks which are conducted to assure consistency of the data reported:

1. Verification of payment data. The monthly payment activity reported by Federal entities on the Statements of Transactions is compared to the payment activity of Federal entities as reported by disbursing officers.

2. Verification of collection data. Reported collections appearing on Statements of Transactions are compared to deposits as reported by Federal Reserve Banks.

### 5. Other Sources of Information About Federal Government Financial Activities

- A Glossary of Terms Used in the Federal Budget Process, 2005 (Available from the U.S. Government Accountability Office, at http://www.gao.gov/new.items/do5734sp.pdf/September, or by calling 202-512-6000. This glossary provides a basic reference document of standardized definitions of terms used by the Federal Government in the budget making process).

- Daily Treasury Statement (Available on the internet at http://www.fms.treas.gov/dts/). The Daily Treasury Statement is published each working day of the Federal Government and provides data on the cash and debt operations of the Treasury.

- Monthly Statement of the Public Debt of the United States (Available on the internet at http://www.treasurydirect.gov/govt/reports/pd/mspd/mspd.htm). This publication provides detailed information concerning the public debt.

- Treasury Bulletin (Available from GPO, Washington, D.C. 20401 on a subscription or single copy and on the internet at http://fms.treas.gov/bulletin/index.html). Quarterly, contains a mix of narrative, tables, and charts on Treasury issues, Federal financial operations, international statistics, and special reports.

- Budget of the United States Government, Fiscal Year 20__ (Available from GPO, Washington, D.C. 20401 on a subscription basis only and on the internet at http://www.access.gpo.gov/usbudget). This publication is a single volume which provides budget information and contains:

    - Appendix, The Budget of the United States Government, FY 20__
    - The United States Budget in Brief, FY 20__
    - Analytical Perspectives
    - Historical Tables

- Combined Statement of Receipts, Outlays, and Balances of the United States Government (Available from Bureau of the Fiscal Services, U.S. Department of Treasury, Washington, D.C. 20227 and on the internet at http://fms.treas.gov/annualreport/index.html). This report includes budgetary results at the summary level and presents individual receipt and appropriation accounts at the detail level.

**Scheduled Release**

**The release date for the June 2014 Statement
will be 2:00 p m. EST July 11, 2014.**

Internet service subscribers can access the current issue of the Monthly Treasury Statement through the
Bureau of the Fiscal Service's website:

http://www fms.treas.gov/mts/index.html